A SECRET STORY OF
miscarriages

ELLIE ROBERTS

SEVEN PREGNANCIES, ONE BABY, AND AN IMAGINARY BUN

Copyright © 2021 by Ellie Roberts

All rights reserved. No part of this book may
be reproduced or used in any manner without
written permission of the copyright owner except
for the use of quotations in a book review.

First edition September 2022

Cover design and formatting by Softwood Self Publishing
Printed by Amazon, UK

ISBN 978-1-8381702-2-6

To all my children.

CONTENTS

PREFACE	7
INTRODUCTION	11
MISCARRIAGE NUMBER ONE: AN UNEXPECTED TURN OF EVENTS	15
MISCARRIAGE NUMBER TWO: SEEKING ANSWERS IN SPAIN	37
THE BABY	54
MISCARRIAGE NUMBER THREE: THE CONFIDENT COUPLE	129
IMAGINARY BUN	153
MISCARRIAGE NUMBER FOUR: LIFE WORK BALANCE	162
MISCARRIAGE NUMBER FIVE: GREAT EXPECTATIONS	181
MISCARRIAGE NUMBER SIX: FOOL'S PARADISE	201
CLOSURE	228
ADOPTION	239
BEING A MUM	249

PREFACE

Why do miscarriages have to be a secret? I have been writing this book for years, but I have only told about ten people about it. My husband thinks the book is a mistake, and of the others who know of it, only two have asked me, just the once, how I was getting on with it. Miscarriage is a taboo subject.

But how many women miscarriage in a year? The Miscarriage Association estimates around a quarter of a million people in the UK. In the six years when I was felt so alone having my miscarriages, I was surrounded by about one and a half million women going through the same thing.

Mine was a hard journey, one that is not typically talked about. But contrary to what I believed at the time, it was not a unique journey. I have since spoken to, or been told of, plenty of other couples in the same situation. Yet everybody keeps quiet about miscarriage as if it were a shameful secret. Your fault. Something you have done wrong. I have heard a woman claim her miscarriage happened because she had been bad in a previous life. A friend once told me she did not want to hear about my story because it could be bad luck for her own pregnancies.

A miscarriage is not shameful; we should not feel we must keep silent, especially as we desperately need new medical research; both myself and my mother-in-law, who suffered several miscarriages in the 1970s, went through the same tests and were offered the same solutions: nothing new, almost forty years apart.

I was never offered any psychological help or referred to the NHS or a private group for counselling. A study by Imperial College published in 2016 states how women who have suffered miscarriages are at risk of post-traumatic stress disorder (PTSD) and many of them will suffer from anxiety problems. While it's great that a study was done, I could have told them as much for free. Why did they not know about it until then? Is it because women do not complain? We go home, lock our front doors, and cry in silence in the privacy of our homes. Well, maybe it is time to shout out loud. I have known a colleague move jobs after a stillbirth (pregnancy loss from week twenty-four of gestation). She could not cope with people knowing about it at work; it was too painful. Another co-worker moved to another country to try to forget, too traumatised to try for a baby again after a lack of medical explanation for her situation. I never saw her smile in all the time I worked with her.

I do not want the miscarriages to define my life, although they are a poignant measure of who I am. It hurts to talk about it, but it hurts more *not* to talk about it. My babies have no voice; *I* am their voice.

Why did I write this book?

I decided to write this book out of a desire to help. That

is my reason. I am not willing to share my story per se. I do not intend to make anybody cry or feel sorry for me. There are more terrible stories in the world in these times.

The idea of the book came to me when I was looking for information regarding reasons for miscarriage and how to produce a successful pregnancy next time and found none. I could only buy books about joyful pregnancies, cheerful journals, how to decorate the nursery room safely, and about a loopy, amazing, intense life with your little pitty-patty toddler and DIY daddies. I found one American book after my third miscarriage. On the first page, it said that lots of women have only one miscarriage; two miscarriages are improbable; three are so rare you should not worry about it happening to you.

I wish I had made myself heard when I had so many unanswered questions. I wish I'd had more medical knowledge at the time and had been able to challenge some of the supposed 'facts' I was given during upsetting moments – facts that turned out to be incorrect. I wish I had been able to stop and calm down.

Women are not alone, women have power; we simply are not taught how to use it. My overwhelming self-doubt and my amateur knowledge of medical subjects always froze my speech during the most upsetting moments, when the pain of loss took over and the well-formed sentences in my mind were never spoken out loud.

I am sharing my story to let you know you are not alone

and maybe also to offer a new perspective, to help you look for different solutions and alternatives.

If, by writing this book, I can help one single person to keep strong, to challenge preconceptions, to be proactive, to feel better about themselves, to breathe slowly and keep moving, my objective will be achieved.

If you are going through a painful miscarriage, I share your pain. Please do not let anybody belittle you. Take good care of yourself and be sure you sort out any issues in your life – pregnancy-related or not – in your best personal interest. Be sure to remain in control of your life. Be strong and love yourself. Ask for a second opinion or a third; listen to your body, do what is best for you. Believe in yourself.

INTRODUCTION

When I was a child, I enjoyed going down to the port in my Spanish hometown; large freighters from Hong Kong used to moor there. I could see them from the far distance if I looked out of my grandmother's kitchen window, while dreaming that I was going to marry a Chinese man (later substituted for a German man) and have twelve children: six girls and six boys, plus twenty-five dogs – like a farmer in my paternal grandmother's village. I was no more than five years old when I was expressed this, but I can still hear my voice and sense the determination of a little person with a big plan.

After growing up listening to my violent father through closed doors, with fear as my main companion, my teenage self decided never to get married or have children; however, I intended to adopt a Chinese girl at the earliest opportunity after reading an article about baby girls being thrown into the river in some countries, for no other reason than their being female. That was my life plan. The dog idea, if considerably scaled down, remained.

While at university, the plan was still firmly in place: I was never going to marry or have my own children, although, somehow, I was looking forward to becoming a grandmother and cuddling and spoiling lots of little grandchildren. I didn't go into the technical details that would enable my future grandmother status. In the meantime, my own grandmother bought a dog, which she loved dearly. Once, when she was, unusually, rather annoyed with her own grownup offspring, she told me that dogs were better behaved than children and caused you less sorrow.

After finishing university in Spain, I could not see any real prospects of finding a job. The unemployment rate was nearly twenty-five per cent, doubling for young people. My only realist option was to join the thousands of hopefuls preparing for exams to become a civil servant for the few positions that opened once a year.

I considered a two-year postgraduate course to obtain a qualification in Politics and International Relations, offered at Barcelona University, which could have given me access to positions within the EU institutions. However, further study depended on my parents forking all the expenses (there are no grants or loans in Spain for students or part-time jobs to help with money). My father, well known for his hate of Catalan institutions, made clear he was in charge, since it was his money. I should do exactly as he wanted if he was going to support me financially. I should buy and eat the food he approved of and I would not be allowed to go out with friends in the evening.

There was only one way forward. I wanted to do my own thing, live by myself under my own rules. I considered moving either to Paris or London. My French was not great, and some research indicated that it was easier to get a job in London. London was such a cool option. I loved watching

MTV, and I dreamt of getting a job as a presenter there. I only made it to the front door on a trip to Camden.

It took me a few months of saving up any money that came to me, from birthdays and Christmas. I was baby-sitting my neighbours' child and I sat on poll tables for 12 hours on election days, which gave me a precious fifty pounds.

But I was petrified of buying a one-way plane ticket to London. I walked many days to the travel agency to stop at their front door and come back home. One day, while in my room, I said to myself 'yes or no', decide now and forever, while walking towards the radio, which was tuned into a vintage music station. I switched it on to hear 'Last Train to London' (the chorus from the Electric Light Orchestra song).

This helped me make my decision. I moved to London. I was twenty-four years old. I had three suitcases (one of them even had wheels), no mobile phone, no email address, no job, and no place to live. Within a couple of months, I was settled, I had a job, and I was loving every minute of my new life.

After having my years of fun, independence, and career progress, I moved to Edinburgh to study a master's degree. Love struck right through my heart in the shape of a Norwegian Viking.

The relationship was not meant to last for a lifetime. My heart got badly broken. It was my birthday, five days to Christmas Day and I was in Oslo with my Norwegian boyfriend, when suddenly it clicked. He didn't love me. It wasn't anything specific he said. I just added up all the things he'd said, along with the things he hadn't said. A REM song – 'Everybody Hurts' – was playing at the bar. I haven't been able to bear listening to that song since that moment, which I believed at the time could not possibly be any sadder. A few days later, we had a conversation. I wanted an unrealistic level of commitment from him that I knew we didn't have, but in my desperation, I had to try. He was quick to say he was not interested in any further commitment. In retrospective, my infatuation was not only about him. He was a good guy, but it was the rest of his friends over there and the style of life in Norway, which made the whole package so desirable to me.

Three years later – my heart mended and working in London again – I met Michael at a dinner party. I knew he was the one from that first night, when we chatted for over three hours over our meal, accompanied by couple bottles of Spanish wine.

It was early days in our relationship when I went for a trip to visit my family back in Spain, so I kept my new attachment private. My mother took me out for a coffee; she had decided to have a 'talk'. She told me, 'You have tried so hard yet failed to find a man. You've always failed. I don't think you are ever going to manage to be with somebody. But don't you worry, darling. There are many good things about being single in life. Many good things indeed, and you'll have to get used to enjoying them.'

This was when my secret history of miscarriages began.

MISCARRIAGE NUMBER ONE
An Unexpected Turn of Events

On our third date, Michael drove to my place to pick me up for a day out. He owned an enormous Mercedes that he was very proud of.

'What do you think?' he asked. 'Big enough for all our children?'

'Looks like it,' I replied, glancing at the backseat.

'So, do I have a girlfriend?'

'I don't know, you've not asked yet.'

'Well, would you like to be my girlfriend?'

'Yes.'

He drove me to his home later that day to say hello to Treacle, his cat. I'd heard worse excuses and decided I liked them both.

A few months later, we moved in together. Treacle approved of the change. She took to sitting between us on the sofa to remind me who was the boss, though.

I changed my job. I went from working at a university as a web developer to working for the public sector as a web manager. It was a much sought-after promotion. I was on a high; however, I missed my old colleagues enormously from day one, as well as the friendly academic environment that I used to take for granted during my working day.

I became the manager of a man who'd applied not only for my position (which he had held on an interim basis for six months), but for over twenty other managerial jobs – as I was duly informed in my first week. George, my web assistant, welcomed me with harsh comments such as, 'Aren't you ashamed of being Spanish after what Columbus and Pizarro did in South America in 1495?' and 'My previous manager was better than you'.

My own boss, who would have chosen a monkey over George as a web manager, kept me on my toes too. After a few glasses of wine during our departmental Christmas lunch, she told me: 'I don't like foreign people. I think I'm going to move to France to avoid living with that many foreigners.' I considered mentioning she would be a foreigner herself in France and she would be surrounded by even more foreigners and a lack of many English people. I decided against it. It was still early days; nevertheless, I had the impression it was an office where nobody stayed for longer than strictly necessary.

In comparison, Michael came across as mature and intelligent, and he was a great boyfriend; we enjoyed each other's company. Early on in our relationship, we had a couple of conversations in which we agreed that – yes! – we'd both like to have children in the future. That was the extent of the discussion. It was enough for me, since, while I wasn't interested in getting involved with a man who didn't want to have children, the 'when' was not an issue yet. I was in no hurry, although I was in my mid-thirties. My career, enjoying life, plus settling down were top of my list.

After a few months at work, it was clear the atmosphere in the office was never going to improve. I was troubled there. Career-wise, it was advisable to keep my job for at least a couple more years. Maybe, I reflected, it was an appropriate time to weigh up the idea of having a baby and then move jobs afterwards.

I had attended a conference about women and careers while working at the university a couple of years earlier. The advice was – suggested by a panel of women-only speakers – to avoid talking about children, deny having a partner or husband, and, above all, do not dare to wear an engagement ring to a job interview. Companies do not want to hire women who are considering having children or have commitments. (In an interview once I was told it was not a good idea to continue with my Italian course one evening a week. Going out with colleagues or friends was fine, but not studying after work.)

Keeping that insightful advice in mind, I figured out I should have a baby while at my current company. I didn't much care what they thought of me or if they made me redundant for having a baby – for instance, by an 'internal company restructure'. I wanted out anyway. I also had a plan B: to look for a new job as soon as the summer was over, then spend some time settling into a new company and a senior role before getting pregnant. Either way, it was time to consider my immediate future and take steps.

I needed to tackle the issue with Michael, and what a better time to do it than during a marvellous beach holiday?

The not-so-enjoyable holiday.

Getting pregnant, accidentally or willingly, was not an option I had ever considered in any of my previous relationships. While not always the most careful person, apart from a one-off morning-after-pill shopping trip to be 200 per cent sure, I had managed my pregnancy-free existence pretty well.

When Michael and I started going out, I wasn't keen on taking the pill again. I'd had enough years of it, starting in my late teens as a result of unruly acne. Michael didn't want me on the pill either, 'because it makes women very hormonal'. I guess that is the advantage of having an experienced boyfriend with (I guess) previous hormonal girlfriends.

I figured out we could use a fertility monitor in reverse: a couple trying for a baby would look for a 'happy face' icon or a red dot (depending on the monitor) to indicate the woman was ovulating; therefore, it was a fertile day to try for a baby. A red dot or smiley face for us meant 'do not have unprotected sex' – to avoid a pregnancy. A green dot or no smiley face would indicate a safe day in our case.

It worked fine for the first few months. I saw my ovulation days periodically. After about six months, I started missing the smiley face and the device could not tell me when it was a fertile day. I bought a second monitor, a different brand, wondering whether the first one could be faulty. It was the same result. Both devices either found a fertile day on the same day in a given month or both failed to show an ovulation day. For four months, on two different occasions, I didn't have any fertile days, according to both monitors.

That lack of smiley combined with the fact that for over two years my periods had been getting shorter, from five days down to sometimes only one morning, I was concerned I was going through an early menopause. I asked my uncle, a pharmacist, for advice. He didn't believe both monitors could be faulty or that I was not ovulating. 'It sounds more like a hormonal problem,' he suggested. I wanted to talk to a doctor about it and decided to book an appointment with a gynaecologist when I visited my family in Spain during the summer.

My working life as a web manager was unpleasant. I was always walking on eggshells and had numerous meetings in an attempt to keep the peace – or the appearance of it – between my boss and George. Gossip was rife. I loved the web work tremendously, but I found it a nuisance that the daily pettiness induced low productivity.

I was looking forward to completing a large project, which involved moving the external website and the intranet to a new content management system. It had kept me working overtime during the week and at weekends for several months. I didn't mind the hard work; it was exciting and a fantastic experience to add to my CV. However, I became so used to being by myself at the office that, one lonely Sunday, when I heard a voice behind me, asking whether I would like a coffee, I jumped out of my desk and screamed.

The marvellous news was that my bitter assistant had resigned. George had accumulated four weeks' annual leave and had waited until the day before an even more demanding project was about to start to give me his resignation letter – two minutes before five o'clock, once he had changed into his running clothes to go home. He announced with a grin, 'I'm going to be on annual leave during my notice period' and left. I loved it. We all loved it. It was a relief for everyone in the department, including him. George's leaving left me on my own with the promise of a temp, who never seemed to arrive despite the pile of work accumulating on my desk.

Despite all the issues, I cared about what I was doing. On top of that, some of my colleagues were fantastic. I got on with working life. I had a schedule: work hard for a couple of months and then enjoy a nice summer holiday; by the end of summer, get on with either looking for a job or having a baby if the 'conversation' went well.

In the middle of the work chaos, Michael and I had sex one night – after months without finding a fertile day. The following morning, the evasive smiley looked at me from the stick. I was surprised. 'Oops! We'll need to be careful tonight.' I was too exhausted to speculate any further about smileys and forgot all about it.

The day my period was due, nothing happened, even though I had always been 100 per cent regular. Another day and another went by, and I kept on counting. Still, it didn't cross my mind that I could be pregnant; on the contrary, I claimed, 'The menopause is here! Or maybe,' I reasoned, 'I'm too exhausted to have a period.' It had never been the case before. All the same, I had read it could happen to women.

We were about to go on our summer holiday to sunny Mauritius. I was looking forward to the trip, my choice. One day after work, I went shopping, but clothes in my usual size didn't fit me around my waist, which was disappointing since I had been working out at the gym during my lunch hour to look good in my swimming costume. At this point, my period was two weeks late. I could see it was time to buy a pregnancy test, but I couldn't find the right moment to do it.

A few days later, we were at the airport. I still hadn't mentioned anything about a possible pregnancy to Michael. My brother was forever telling his girlfriend he couldn't cope with the female obsession around the 'I may be pregnant, I may not pregnant drama' every time there was a period delay or doubts on the efficiency of the contraceptive methods. He'd asked her to only tell him when she had physical undisputed evidence that she was pregnant. I went for that same approach. I was sure, anyway, that I was not pregnant. Who? Me? Pregnant? No way.

At the airport, I went into Boots to buy a pregnancy

test. On the hypothetical off-chance that I *was* pregnant, I shouldn't be drinking cocktails during the holiday; I should be responsible. I knew I should check at this point. The store was crowded, with long queues at the tills. Queuing annoys me, so I decided not to bother. Instead, I would look for a pharmacy in Mauritius as soon as we landed.

When we arrived in Mauritius, it looked postcard pretty. It was a perfect holiday island, with lots of trees, flowers, sunny weather, and people wearing summer clothes. On the not-so-positive side, the hotel was in the middle of nowhere, and clearly there were no pharmacies on offer. I hadn't seen any pharmacies at the airport either or on our drive to the hotel. I could buy a cuddly dodo but not a pregnancy test.

The hotel had a spa, which I was eager to try out, so I went there the morning after we arrived. I was given a questionnaire to fill in before I could take any treatments. I stared at one of the questions for minutes: 'Are you pregnant?' *What should I say?* I considered answering that I was not sure – actually, I could be. *I hope I am not since I still need to have the 'conversation' with Michael and maybe I would like to change jobs before thinking of babies. However, if I were pregnant, I would be okay with it; I would never go for a termination only because it was an unplanned pregnancy.*

In the end, I ticked: 'No, I am not.' I concluded I wouldn't be allowed any treatments if I were. I did not realise, in any case, that a spa treatment could be a risk during the early stages of pregnancy. The naivety of the inexperienced person.

I have replayed this moment a thousand times in my mind. I cannot forgive myself for my recklessness, even if it was based on a lack of knowledge rather than anything else. How could I be such an ignorant person?

I settled for a two-hour lymphatic drainage massage, focusing on getting rid of liquid retention on my increasingly round abdomen.

The next day, we went on a day excursion to a natural park with beautiful water lilies and impressive indigenous trees. I took hundreds of pictures. When we arrived back at the hotel, fatigue overwhelmed me. My body was suddenly exhausted. My legs refused to move, and even walking to the swimming pool area was too much of an effort. I lay down on the bed for a rest.

After a couple of hours' rest, I went to the toilet. At that instant, the ordeal started. Blood, blood, and more blood running out of my body. In a moment, a question of seconds, I saw more blood than in a normal, regular period. I remember with sadness my reaction the first time I saw it: *This blood looks different from my normal period blood. It looks like blood made to carry life – bright red, shiny, heavy.* In fact, it was.

I was still in denial. A lot of blood, indeed; maybe it was because of the long delay before my period? No pain, just blood. I placed two pads on top of each other, but I had to replace them every hour because the blood was continuously flowing. I needed to change my underwear, my clothes, the bed sheets continually. It was frightening and I started to feel nervous.

After days of continuous bleeding, I got sick with an ear infection and needed to see a doctor to get antibiotics. We went to the main town on the island to pop into a doctor's surgery recommended by our hotel. I considered asking the GP there about my bleeding. The doctor was keen on an under-the-desk fee for the consultation, no invoice and no questions asked. We didn't mind; my earache was too severe. We bought some antibiotics and then ran for it because he didn't inspire us with confidence.

After three days of heavy bleeding, with no sign of it slowing down, I had to admit that something was not right; this was presumably a miscarriage.

I told Michael. He dismissed my fears straightaway: 'It's surely nothing to worry about. We've been careful and you shouldn't be pregnant.' I was getting niggly with him by that point. Later that day, we got into an argument over something completely irrelevant – his ex's hairdo. Michael got wound up about it, and I became angry with him. 'I might be having a miscarriage here, but you don't seem to care – you're more bothered about your ex's hair!' I told him. I stormed out to sit in the garden. It was late evening, the perfect time for mosquitoes. I got bitten all over and my legs were itching dreadfully.

An edgy atmosphere was taking over, spoiling the holiday. I started pondering what happens to a woman when she is pregnant. *When does a baby start looking like a baby? How soon does it become big?* I was clueless; those reproductive system lessons in junior school seemed long ago. *What happens if a woman has a miscarriage, and how long does it take? Is it painful?* I was not in pain. I was holding on to the lack of pain. *It must just be a bad period.* In movies, miscarriage always looks so distressing.

I was not sure what to do. After our visit to the local doctor, I suspected going to a hospital was not going to be reassuring; I presumed I would be better off at a hospital in London. There were still no pharmacies we could find. I was hoping for the bloody experience to finish soon. At that point, I came to the realisation that it might be better not to know the cause of this bleeding. I didn't want to consider the options. I wanted it to finish and dissolve quietly as soon as possible, right there – on a remote island far away from my daily life. I would make sure in the future I didn't complain about queuing in shops. *If there is a next time*, I analysed. *I will check straightaway whether that is the case.* I had learnt my lesson. If it ended then, by itself, in Mauritius, we would let it be without asking questions. But that was not going to be.

After several days, the blood still showed no sign of slowing down, and heavy clots started to come out. I could hold them with my fingers, soft but firm like gelatine.

We landed back in London on a Saturday night. On Sunday morning, I decided I didn't want to wait until Monday to see a GP. I was uneasy about my wellbeing, not sure of what was happening to my body. I feared becoming seriously ill. I sat down to rub my forehead to consider the situation; I was unwell, tired, feeling odd and nervous, although still not in pain. Medical attention should give us some answers.

We went to the Walk in Centre at the nearest hospital to us, St George's in Tooting, South London. There, I was told I needed to have a pregnancy test and to 'go back home, get a test at the supermarket, and come back to hospital, to the Early Pregnancy Unit, if it's positive'.

Could I be still pregnant after bleeding so much? I didn't think it could be possible at this late stage, after more than ten days of heavy bleeding. *But what do I know about pregnancies anyway?* I was in total panic, realising I had wasted over ten days when I could have been *saving* my baby. Plan or unplanned – this was my baby. I had no doubt that I wanted it if the test was going to show that I was pregnant.

We stopped at the supermarket on our way back home. We bought the test, quickly drove home, and I used it. It was positive. Stupidly enough, I was certain that now the pregnancy had been confirmed and I was back in London, the outcome was going to be okay.

However, not all of us were thinking the same thing. Michael was calm and composed. He asked me: 'Well, this is an unplanned pregnancy. What do you want to do about it?' It hurt like a stab as I hadn't expected the question. In my fairy tale movie, we would both be thrilled I was pregnant and be on our way to see the local magician, I mean doctor, who was going to save our beautiful baby. Michael never said he didn't want the baby.

I realise now that Michael was as shocked as I was. He likes organising things with plenty of time to spare, meditating about them before making a move, whereas I am more of an impulsive person.

My head was spinning with guilt – for not looking for help earlier, for not buying a pregnancy test weeks before, for not telling the spa that I might be pregnant. I could hardly breathe for heart-breaking grief about the possible loss of my baby. A depressing sense of loneliness and loss combined in my head. We needed to go back to hospital. Surely, I imagined, it was realistically too late, but with neither of us having any medical knowledge, we could only go to the Early Pregnancy Unit to await for what the doctors could tell us.

We jumped back in the car to go to hospital. Guilt was killing me inside. I was overwhelmed; it was all too much to deal with. *Why didn't I do anything about it much earlier? Why didn't I check I was pregnant when I should have?* The thoughts were whirling round my head. Michael switched on the radio; there that song was again, 'Everybody Hurts' by R.E.M., always appearing in the lowest moments of my life: The sadness of my heart being broken in Norway disappeared for good there and then. The song remains associated with very painful moments.

We arrived at the hospital after a few minutes. The Early Pregnancy Unit looked quiet and empty. I was mortified I was going to be asked why it had taken me so long to seek medical help. How was I going to explain that I had been bleeding heavy clots for days and let it be, not even checking whether I was pregnant or not? I had no excuse.

When we arrived, I was given a form to fill in. The first question at the top of the page, in big bold letters was: 'Are you single, married, or a widow?' Underneath were three enormous tick boxes. No more options. In my humble opinion, it was more likely that a woman attending the Early Pregnancy Unit had a partner than that she was a widow.

I said to Michael that I was going to tick married. 'Single' implied I was some sort of irresponsible single woman sleeping around, on top of not being careful. He replied, 'No, you have to tick single.' He did not mean any harm. He was technically right, but it hurt. Why was my marital status the most important question to the hospital? Whatever personal circumstances, all pregnant women should have access to the same treatment. On a sore note of personal reflection, if the man who had made me pregnant thought the right thing to do was to tick single, if the correct action to do was to tick single, and if I was single, I ought to acknowledge to myself that I was the only single or non-single person in that hospital interested in the outcome of that pregnancy and that I was completely on my own when losing my baby.

I considered adding an 'in a relationship' box, if it was clinically that important for the hospital to know the marital status of a pregnant lady. In the twenty-first century, it's not such a radical idea to be pregnant and not married.

The non-existent real foetus.

I'd had hardly any first-hand experience of hospitals before this current visit. Only one appointment at a private hospital when I was in my twenties in Spain. Last time I had been severely sick, I was six years old and had chicken pox. I'd enjoyed a week in bed without having to go to school.

The NHS reports in the national press had been consistently alarming – low standards, lack of beds, not enough consultants, endless hours of waiting at A&E. Thus, when we arrived back in hospital, on a Sunday morning with no appointment, and we were told a doctor would see us promptly and that I was going to have an ultrasound scan, we were pleased.

First, we saw a lovely sister – part of the nursing management team in the hospital, not a nun as I first assumed. She listened to me, and she was kind. On the other hand, when the doctor appeared, she took a different approach. She was junior, inexperienced, a confident know-it-all cookie. She listened neither to me nor the sister, who on several occasions tried to talk to her only to be shushed. I had an ultrasound scan, after which the doctor asserted, 'There is nothing there.' It was not a pleasant meeting, but I was relieved. I appreciated the ordeal was over at least. I would not have to deal with it any further – no operations, no added health problems, no drugs needed. Nothing further from reality.

The next Tuesday morning, I woke up early with terrible pains that kept coming and going, making it difficult to walk. It felt like I was going to have the most gruesome diarrhoea of my life. I kept going to the toilet, when I was able to walk. Nothing was coming out. I had to wait in the bathroom for minutes when the pain didn't allow me return to bed. The ache was intermittent; I could see that I was having about ten to fifteen minutes intervals when I would feel fine. During one of those breaks, I drove to the supermarket to purchase a pregnancy test. I was back at home within seven minutes. Acceptance of my loss was too hard to bear. I wanted to believe maybe there was still life hidden somewhere in the blurred cavities of my body.

The test was still positive, like the one I had done the previous Sunday. It showed I was still pregnant. Therefore, somehow, I *was* pregnant, I reckoned. It sounds dumb, when I now know how long it takes for the hormones to go back to normal. At the time, I believed what I needed to believe to keep me going and not break down in pieces.

I sat in the kitchen at the breakfast table, wondering if somehow everything was going to be all right. I wanted salvation for my baby. After about six to seven hours of strong pain and, by now, fourteen days of heavy bleeding, something ran down from inside my body and plopped out into my underwear. It was solid, large, thick. I was scared my body was now breaking into pieces: *could it be a piece of my uterus breaking down?* I ran upstairs to the toilet to check what it was – and there it lay on the cold floor: my tiny baby, with arms, legs, an enormous mouth, closed eyes, both arms bent, touching the cheeks on its face. I could see clearly the silhouette of its left hand with five fingers. A small placenta came out five minutes later. That was – and will certainly remain for the rest of my life – my most shocking, heart-breaking moment. There it was; my dead baby.

I went to the computer to check images of a foetus that age, about ten to twelve weeks. Everything matched, from appearance to size, to the enormous mouth at that stage of development. I have never cried this much in my life. The pain after seeing my dead baby was indescribable. After the foetus appeared, no more blood came out. It had held in there until the last drop of blood to hang onto had been shed. Afterwards, it fell down to oblivion. Perpetually gone.

I could not bring myself to touch it with my hands. I left it on my knickers on the cold bathroom floor. I looked for an empty shoebox. I couldn't just place it in there on its own. I looked for some nice tissue paper, hoping, somehow in my imagination, he or she would notice that I loved him. A desperate, last-minute action to compensate for all that I did not do when I had the chance to change the outcome. There was nothing more I could do for my baby.

There was only one distant witness to that moment, if we can call our neighbours' dog, Daisy, a witness. She was listening on the other side of the wall. Since that day – nobody else knows about this – she has taken to running up and licking me all over every time she sees me, to the bafflement of everyone, who wonder why she has this humongous love and sympathy for me. We will keep it as our little private moment.

I feared I was going insane with sorrow. I called Michael at work. He packed his bag and rushed back home.

How did the hospital respond when we phoned them? That I was imagining things. It was, most likely, only some dried blood. We both wanted it to be analysed because it could have given us some clues – which would have been needed in view of future events. They said no. Was there any private hospital or lab where we could take it? They did not know; worst of all, they did not want to know. Any advice on what to do? 'Put it in the loo and flush it'.

I asked Michael to deal with the box by himself. I could not face knowing what happened to it. I did not want it in the garden. I didn't want the garden to become a mausoleum, or worse, put it there for one of the local foxes to dig it up and eat.

Endless times, I have imaged myself grabbing the box and going to the hospital with the foetus to look for the doctor who scanned me, to ask the hospital staff to tell me to my face that *this* was not a foetus. Regrettably, I was too shocked to think straight at the time; ultimately, I believed that was not going to give me the answers I was looking for. Nonetheless, we should have kept it in the freezer to give us time to calm down and look for a private lab that could do some tests, if nothing else.

The following year, I asked two senior gynaecologists, one of them with links to the same hospital, how it was possible that the doctor had missed the foetus. They replied in the same way: she was inexperienced. No other explanation, no other reason to justify how she'd missed it.

I enquired if it could have been an ectopic pregnancy (meaning the foetus had implanted itself in the fallopian tubes, outside the uterus); therefore, maybe it was not possible to be see it during an ultrasound scan. I was told this was impossible, since the foetus came out by itself, without medical intervention. That does not occur in ectopic pregnancies, the doctors explained; the woman always needs an operation to remove the foetus because it is stuck in the thin fallopian tubes.

A few days later, the hospital called. They wanted to see me again for a second scan to be sure there were no other remains of the pregnancy left behind. I considered whether it was worth going back there. In the end, I went for the scan anyway, hoping for some medical advice. I asked the technician who saw me what I could do to avoid having another miscarriage. She looked at me with disdain, then replied in a loud voice: 'Don't drink, don't smoke, be healthy. It happens all the time. It may happen to you again.' Famous last words.

The hospital wanted to do a blood test to check my iron levels after the miscarriage. A medical student was taking the blood samples, and as she could not find my elusive vein, she got frustrated. In the end, she stabbed me with the needle. I left the hospital feeling dizzy as I sat down to wait for a bus back home. Defeated.

Back at home, I noticed a nasty taste of ink in my mouth. I went to a mirror to look at my tongue. It was dark blue, as if I had broken a pen in my mouth and sucked the ink. I didn't want to find out what it was about. I had no energy left. I let it be.

The aftermath.

Once the hurricane had passed, it was time to deal with the damage; what next? Where were Michael and I in our relationship? It was unlucky I'd got pregnant before having the 'conversation' about it. The unexpected experience had put us in a bad place. It was not easy to talk calmly about having children while remembering our dead baby in the shoebox.

I did not always understand Michael's passiveness during that time. His lack of openness. I wanted a reaction like mine: hopelessness, despair, anger. Yet, from a practical point of view, two hysterical people were not going to get far. We were both mourning in a different way. It took Michael years to be able to talk about it, to express his feelings of loss.

The devastating consequences of the affair extended to all parts of my life. After the miscarriage, my body was not working well, physically or mentally. When my period started again, twenty-six days from the day the foetus came out, it didn't stop for over six weeks, until I had an appointment with the gynaecologist in Spain – I wasn't sure where to go in London; furthermore, private doctors in London are at least four times more expensive than in Spain. I was given drugs to regulate the hormones. They worked well and my periods were back to normal by the end of the summer.

I had no rest. The pain of guilt was overwhelming – to this day, I still believe the spa trip was the cause of it. In any case, I should have checked whether I was pregnant or not. The image of the tiny little baby haunts me. I did not have a clue what to do to help myself. I felt I needed advice – professional support. Talking about it was not going to cure me. I did not want to feel sorry for myself. I was in an awfully dark place; I was seeking something out of the box that could give me the strength I could not find in myself.

I had read in women's magazines how amazing acupuncture could be. Not in my wildest dreams had I imagined having it myself. I was – and still remain – needle phobic. I believed at the time that it was nothing more than a current fad or witchcraft, rather than anything else; that there was nothing better than Western medicine.

There was a lady called Kylie Box who practised acupuncture at my gym. I booked a session. I told her that I wasn't sure why I was there, or how she could help me, or even what sort of help I was looking for.

Kylie asked me many questions about my life, including my general health. When I told her I had suffered from constipation issues for about ten years, she affirmed she could sort that out quickly. At this point, I highly regretted booking the appointment. I wanted to leave immediately and not go ahead with my session. However, I didn't want to make a scene by running out of the treatment room, so I went through with it.

Miracles do happen sometimes. As Kylie had claimed, she sorted out my lack of trips to the toilet within a click of the fingers – or, rather, a few pricks. On the grounds of this unexpected success, I saw her two more times to be sure I remained toilet trained.

Despite the physical success, I did not experience any improvement regarding my grief. On my third session, Kylie told me acupuncture could help with pregnancies. At that moment, although she was lovely and professional, I decided she was surely mad. I was not going to see her again. I left it there.

MISCARRIAGE NUMBER TWO
Seeking Answers in Spain

After the disappointment of the miscarriage and the whole unnerving experience that came with it, the warm summer and some downtime were welcome. We had endured a nightmare, and we had survived. I told myself the miscarriage was my fault because of the strong massage I'd had in Mauritius. Although doctors seemed to dismiss it, I'd read that massage techniques have been used to induce abortions for centuries. The general message coming towards me from the medical profession, friends, and family was that there had been something wrong with the foetus; therefore, what had happened was for the best.

Michael and I had a heart-warming conversation over lunch one late summer day, at one of our favourite pubs in Wandsworth. We accepted we had been through a horrible and unlucky experience. We both wished to have children and we were willing to give it a go straightaway.

We devised a working plan, starting with my taking it easy at work; no more getting stressed now that there were no big projects ahead. No massages from now on. Have a baby. Go on maternity leave. Get a new job.

Getting pregnant was easy, achieved within a month. This time, we used the ovulation monitors for the *when*-to-get-pregnant business that they were intended for, rather than our previous approach.

When my period was late, I was ecstatic. I counted each day, all the way to a week. I told Michael, on day seven, I believed I was pregnant. He replied, 'What are you waiting for? Buy a pregnancy test!' We went to purchase one together. My heart was beating hard – oh joy! It was a positive result. I was pregnant.

I remember going to work the following morning, walking across the common. I was wearing a long skirt that brushed against the long autumn grass. I was the happiest person on earth. I felt immensely grateful, truly fortunate. Life had given me the opportunity to put things right.

My joy did not linger very long. Two weeks later, while walking back to my office after a meeting half a mile away, an awful pain low down in the centre of my abdomen paralysed me. It was deep and horrid. There was a fist inside my abdomen pressing hard on one single point. I had to stop walking to catch my breath. It lasted for about five minutes. Afterwards, the pain was gone as quick as it came. I went to the loo when I entered my building and there was a spot of blood. *It could not be happening again.*

It was a Friday afternoon. I called the GP surgery and managed to get an appointment for later that day after work. I left work promptly to go for my consultation. I told the doctor I would like to have an ultrasound scan. He said no, that was not the normal practice on the NHS; no scans for pregnant women. I could have one scan in week twelve and a further one in week twenty; that was all.

I asked him, 'What should I do if I start bleeding again?'

He shrugged, then replied, 'If you keep bleeding, this is a miscarriage.'

His response was rather poor, I thought.

I went back home. There was no more bleeding since the initial bleed that afternoon. The weekend went without incident. I was back at work on Monday, getting on with life.

On Tuesday night, I made a nice dinner at home. I like cooking, and we always have dinner together after work. After no more scares to report since the previous Friday, we were confident all was well. We got talking about the baby: boy or girl? When were we going to tell our friends? After dinner, we moved to the sofa in the living-room. What a joyful family scene, with cat included.

We switched on the TV; Michael was holding my hand. All of a sudden, a stream of blood came down my legs, all the way down to my ankles, reaching my slippers. I ran upstairs to the toilet. It looked bad – blood kept coming out of me as if somebody had opened a tap to let the water run freely. I put on a couple of pads and hurried straight back downstairs. I did not want to waste a minute. We were going to do something immediately.

We called NHS Direct to explain the situation. We were told an 'expert' was going to call us back. We sat down to wait for the call. After about ten minutes, the bleeding stopped.

The tap seemed to be closed. I was not in any pain. I was not sick or weak, only scared.

The wait for the call was taking ages, over an hour, so we decided to go to A&E since we anticipated that was what we would be told to do. We redirected the home number to Michael's mobile, jumped in the car, and went to A&E at St George's.

I filled in the usual form. After a few minutes, a young, dynamic-looking doctor called us. *Looks good,* I told myself. *A young person will be more sympathetic, proactive, more willing to do something than an old doctor.*

I told him: 'I'm pregnant, I'm bleeding. I had a miscarriage five months ago.'

'Well, it may be a miscarriage again.'

'Could I have an ultrasound scan?'

'No, you cannot. If you keep on bleeding, it will be a miscarriage.'

'Could I see an obstetrician or somebody else at the Early Pregnancy Unit?'

'No, there is nothing they can do.'

'Okay, if it is a miscarriage, then I want an ERPC (Evacuation of Retained Products of Conception) – an operation to remove the foetus. I saw the previous foetus coming out and found it a distressful experience.'

'No, we don't do them – a miscarriage is a natural process. Go home, try to forget about it, carry on like normal.'

So much for dynamic young souls and my misguided

prejudices against older doctors. We went back to the car, feeling downcast and hopeless.

We were still on our way back home when the NHS 'expert' called us back two to three hours after our first call. Michael and his fancy gadgets – we answered the phone on the car system and told the caller we were driving but she was on a speaker phone. I explained the situation, the bleeding, my previous miscarriage, the visit to A&E. We told her we desperately needed advice on what to do next. We didn't mind visiting a private hospital in London if she could suggest one to us. We would do anything to save our baby – whether treatment through the NHS or privately, in England or Spain or anywhere else in the world, if only somebody with the expertise we lacked could direct us to the right place.

'Please help us. Give us some hope. Suggest something we could do,' I pleaded.

'Have you been beaten up or raped by your partner? Is that why you are bleeding?'

We looked at each other in disbelief; we were not only speechless but shocked. *If I had been beaten up or raped, I would be talking to the police, not you,* I thought. *Furthermore, without a doubt, not in the car with my attacker, letting him hear my conversation.*

The *expert* recommended that we pay the GP a visit or go back to hospital if I become ill. To be fair, she told us later in the conversation that she was not an expert as such; merely a person working in a call centre and following instructions on her computer screen. If she had to follow a set of questions regardless of what we were telling her, our hope was fading away.

I made a decision while still on the phone; I was going to buy a plane ticket to Spain as soon as we arrived back home. I wanted to see an obstetrician. I wanted to have an ultrasound scan to see how the pregnancy was developing. If the worst came to the worst, I needed to have an operation to save me the pain of seeing my second dead baby. Also, more important, in Spain, a second miscarriage triggers an investigation; therefore, they could do some studies on myself and the foetus. Surely, we would get some answers.

I would have to go private in Spain since I was no longer a resident in the country. I yearned for an explanation. If I had to pay for it, I would. Spain seemed a good compromise since the fees for private doctors would be more reasonable, plus the two-miscarriages policy in the Spanish NHS (Seguridad Social) would avoid any discussions regarding my bad luck rather than looking for an underlying problem. (A woman needs to have three miscarriages in England before investigations, although we later found out that private doctors might carry out an investigation after two miscarriages.)

We arrived back home. I went on my computer to book a ticket to fly to Spain early the next morning and kept my fingers crossed I could arrange a doctor's appointment on the other side. I crossed my fingers that no foetus was going to slip down my legs when I was on the plane.

I left a message for my boss on her work voicemail. I could imagine her thunder face when listening to it. Fortunately, I had booked a week off as a holiday beforehand. I was going to be on sick leave for three days; if I needed more time off, the extra days would be covered by my annual leave.

(Years later, while editing this book, years after the unfortunate call with NHS Direct (now called NHS 111 service), Michael happens to be in bed with a bad back. No point in going to the GP, we know, and it's not bad enough for A&E. I suggested calling the 111 to seek some advice. Michael, who does not want to read this book or be involved in what I am writing, laughed bitterly and responded, 'Yes, they might ask me whether my back is in pain because I have been beaten up by my wife.' He has not forgotten either.)

The Spanish experience.

I made it to the airport and onto the plane the following day. The flight was fine; no pain, no bleeding. Afterwards, I had a two-hour bus ride from the airport to my parents' – technically separated at this time but still cohabiting. I phoned the GP practice and booked an appointment that evening. There had been no more blood since the night before and my body felt okay. Knowing that I was going to see a doctor later in the day slowed down my breathing. My body relaxed while I dreamt the pregnancy was going to be fine after seeing him. The magic pill that was going to make it all right was on its way.

Benigno, my gynaecologist, was pleasant and smiley as usual. His name means 'benign' – what a fantastic name for a doctor. I had known him for about fifteen years, and he had a good reputation in the city. He was the Head of the IVF department at a private hospital in town, along with his own private practice. I had visited him routinely for check-ups and any other gynaecological issues. He was past retirement age, but still cheerfully working. He had the calm manner of somebody who had seen it all before.

He was surprised I couldn't have an ultrasound scan in London. 'The best way to see what's going on is by looking at it,' he asserted. He told me about one of his sons, a junior gynaecologist, who had gone to work in a hospital in Leeds but quit his job because he claimed junior doctors, like himself, were often left in charge of patients with no supervision or anybody to double-check their decisions during weekends and night shifts and had to make life or death decisions without benefitting from the expertise or advice of senior doctors.

After our chat, we moved to the ultrasound room. Every time I have an ultrasound scan with a doctor, I find it hilarious how keen they are to show me what they see: 'This,' they assert, 'is your left ovary. Can you see it here?' And here is some tissue for this and for that …' I swear I can see nothing more than grey and white dots, but they will not take that for an answer. 'Can you see how clear it is now?' they ask. 'Oh yes,' I say (but really, not a chance).

Benigno revealed the embryo was there. He could see something that, to the untrained eye, looked like black circles surrounding the whole embryo sack. Those 'holes' were the damaged tissue where the bleeding had occurred, which confirmed a miscarriage had started.

Benigno felt negative about the outcome, based on over forty years of experience, and asserted it was not looking good. However, he said, 'It's still early days, there is a small hope, if not much.' We should wait for a few days to see if a heartbeat appeared. The bleeding had stopped, and maybe there was a small chance of the pregnancy developing normally. As a result, I felt positive, based on my few weeks of pregnancy, together with my dreamy nature.

I walked back to my parents' house, where I lay in bed as still as a log. I remembered a friend of mine, Lola. Some years back, after she'd had a baby girl, she'd suffered a miscarriage when she was over five months pregnant, which was caused by a weak cervix. Her following pregnancy after the miscarriage was not looking good. She was told to lie in bed day and night without getting up for anything other than to go to the loo. She spent some difficult months in bed but had a healthy boy in the end.

I wondered how it was going to end for me. I was bored. I didn't have much to do. I was too unsettled to read. There was no TV in the room. I listened to the radio all day. Lots of programmes about car maintenance. I laughed, imagining the faces of my friends if they could see me listening to a motor programme.

After a few days, I went back to the clinic for the appointment. During my period of bed rest, there had not been any bleeding; on the negative side, there was some murky stuff coming out persistently. I was still hopeful. Michael, also now on holiday, flew to Spain and came to the clinic with me. Four eager pairs of eyes looked at the screen: Benigno, the nurse, my boyfriend, and me. The embryo had grown but there was no heartbeat. There should have been a heartbeat by then, because of how far into the pregnancy we were and the size of the embryo.

Benigno suggested waiting for three more days. Afterwards, if the pregnancy was not viable, I would have an operation to remove what was there, a standard procedure in Spanish hospitals to avoid further complications, such as sepsis. Benigno was pessimistic, but I remained upbeat. Three more days for a heartbeat. The embryo had grown. To my inexperienced mind, if there was no bleeding, all was fine.

That night, Michael and I went out for dinner to a fancy new French restaurant, where I ate lots of cheese, unaware that some foods, such as soft cheeses and cured meat, are not allowed during pregnancy because of the risk of toxoplasmosis. We talked about the pregnancy, both positive about the potential outcome.

The next morning, I was woken by nausea and abdominal cramps. I remained in my pyjamas, running from the bed to the bathroom and back. I could not stop vomiting.

I wondered about its cause. There were the three usual suspects: food poisoning, pregnancy sickness, or end-of-pregnancy sickness.

When we went back to see the gynaecologist for our next appointment, there was still no heartbeat, no change in size, no development. There was no sign of a placenta developing. It was all over. ERPCs are done in Spain within twenty-four hours of the confirmation of the miscarriage. We arranged to have an ERPC at a private hospital the next day.

One more step in the wrong direction for me in the baby race. I had no compass to guide me to a happy finish line. I was desperate to understand what was going on, for somebody to tell me what I was doing wrong.

I was asked to go to the hospital early the next day with an empty stomach. Benigno mentioned the operation was a quick and easy affair. I would need to be in hospital overnight as a standard procedure. He did not anticipate any further problems. The hospital would be able to analyse the remains of the foetus. At a later stage, I should decide if I wanted to have tests done on me too.

The day did not go as smoothly as I'd hoped. I was perplexed when a priest came into my room – unannounced, uninvited – to offer me support. Spain is a Catholic country, although I have never been a practising Catholic. I have not heard of this type of visit happening anywhere else, including other Spanish hospitals. Anger rose in me when I saw him appear in my room; the last thing I needed was Catholic compassion. I was not married – he did ask – and I did not want a sermon about it or any other decisions in my life.

This happened before the great scandal of stolen babies in Spain made headlines. Maybe the priest was upset he couldn't steal my baby as they had done for years, with nuns and doctors taking babies from single mums or 'inappropriate' couples to give away for adoption to more 'suitable' couples. (However, if I viewed having the priest there as disturbing, the story my grandmother told me a few miscarriages later was more distressing.)

Once he left, two nurses appeared to say they were going to shave my private bits – normal procedure for hospital operations. They lifted the sheet and my gown, separated my legs, and started doing it in full view of Michael. I told them I wanted some privacy and to pull the curtains around the bed to keep me covered from any other uninvited person popping into the room.

Afterwards, one nurse was teaching the other one how to put in a drip. I was the first person to experience her new skill – and it was painful. Then I was given two pills to insert into my vagina. 'It is good for you,' I was told by the nurses. 'It helps with the recovery and will make the whole procedure faster.'

I declined help with inserting the pills and did it myself. It took about thirty minutes for the frightful pain and heavy bleeding to start. The pain was not like in my first miscarriage when the foetus came out by itself in the end. This time, I had no period-style pain or any feeling of diarrhoea. I cannot describe it. There was an all-over constant cramp that made my whole body twist in agony.

My mother appeared in my room, having insisted on being there to help, and although I told her many times – politely – to go, she refused. Then Michael wanted me to hold his hand – rather than biting my arm and sinking my nails into my skin to divert the pain. The ache was too excruciating for hand holding, even for hand squeezing. I asked for painkillers a couple of times. I was told I could have nothing before the operation. It was unbearable, and I kept biting my arms and hands to ease the pain. I couldn't breathe.

After an agonising hour, I got a high fever. I was sweaty and confused. My distress scared the nurses and doctors. Suddenly, I became highly popular, with lots of checks and visits from senior hospital staff. I was given antibiotics and painkillers to try to get the fever down, since it is not possible to operate on a patient with a fever.

After about thirty minutes, I was feeling better. The pain eased and the fever started to go down. I asked Michael to take my mother away for a coffee so I could get some much-needed privacy and quiet. While I was on my own, the nurses came for me, and I was taken to the operating theatre.

It was a cheerful environment. Everybody was chatty and in a good mood. Just before I was put to sleep to get a vacuum up my legs, I was asked which football team I supported; bad luck, they all supported my rival team! The anaesthetist asked me to count to ten. I reached three.

The operation was quick – in and out in twenty minutes. I woke up in the recovery room; somebody came to check I was fine. I momentarily forgot I was in Spain and started replying in English. I saw the puzzled face and promptly changed to Spanish. I was doing okay.

I was taken back to my room. I was by myself, my mother and Michael having decided to go for a bite to eat since they knew it was going to be a long day. I was physically fine, no more pain, but otherwise empty. ERPC patients share the hospital ward with pregnant women in labour. I could hear a woman being wheeled back to her room with her new-born baby. It was all excitement in that room, lots of laughter and cheerful voices. Lots of relatives started arriving to meet the baby. They all laughed and shouted – after all, this was noisy Spain. I could hear the baby crying. I wanted to cry too.

I was alone in the room with my thoughts. ERPC – Evacuation of Retained Products of Conception. What a name to mean 'we are going to vacuum your dead baby out of your body'. (The name was changed in 2013 to SMM, or Surgical Management of Miscarriage, since some women found the ERPC name upsetting.)

At least, I said to myself, if a hospital does not have the capacity to offer an ERPC on the grounds of budget constraints or staff shortage, they should inform the person of the different options and let the person know that you can go to a different hospital. A friend of mine who had a miscarriage was told to put a plastic cover on her bed 'because it might get messy'; another one was left bleeding for over three months, with regular scans to check whether the foetus was still in her body. *How can this be good for anybody, mentally or physically?*

I remembered being told at St George's to 'go home and relax': 'It's a natural thing. Go to work and don't think about it.' Maybe for a doctor with a clinical mind it is only some dead tissue and blood. For me, it was something different. St George's was, I found out later, the worst performing maternity hospital in London and one of the bottom three in the country.

When my mother and Michael came back, she told me she had met, randomly and separately in the street, two women she had known for years, both with several children. My mother mentioned to them I was in hospital and the reason. Both women then revealed to her that they'd had several miscarriages, one of them three, the other five, before having their children. They had never told anybody about it. Silent grieving.

I had to spend the night in hospital. I was not in any pain; I would have liked to go home. My left hand hurt because of the drip, but it could not be removed in case I got a fever again. I was given dinner after a day without food, which was welcome. I didn't manage to eat well with my right hand – being a lefty. Michael helped me to cut up the food. After my dinner, he had to leave for the night. I was relieved the experience was over, trusting the analysis of the foetus could give us some clues. I was feeling useless. I did not seem to be able to do something that was so plain easy for other women.

The next morning, after a check-up, I was allowed to go home. No fever, no pain. I could walk alright, if a bit cautiously.

Michael asked me what I wanted to do. 'Do you need to lie down?'

'No,' I said. 'I need to move, I need to escape.'

We went for a long walk and for lunch; anything would do, as long as I did not have to sit down and think about what had happened.

By the afternoon, I had thought of some new questions for Benigno. We popped into his private clinic without phoning for an appointment. I wanted to talk about what to do next and how long I needed to wait to get pregnant again. Benigno seemed concerned to see me walking around and said I should be resting at home. I was confused about this, as he himself had mentioned it was a quick and easy operation. He still wanted me to rest for a few days. I didn't tell him we were off early the next morning, both of us having to go back to work the following week.

We asked Benigno what we should do if I kept having miscarriages. He suggested considering IVF (in vitro fertilisation) if we could not find a conclusive reason. Michael and I spoke about it. We were both sure it was not a route we wanted to consider, for many reasons: success rates are not that high; we are friends with couples who have gone down that route and had heard how expensive and stressful it is;

a friend of Michael's had lost twins in the late stages of her pregnancy after losing another boy in a first IVF pregnancy. She eventually had a baby boy. There were lots of articles in magazines about it, and the whole experience sounded overwhelming. I had no doubt that it was not for me.

The next day, we started our long returning trip to London. We started from the north-west part of Spain with a four-hour train journey to take our flight from Madrid. While in Madrid, before going to the airport, we visited one of my brothers who lived there. He had a three-month-old daughter – my goddaughter. I was fine seeing her; she was such a small baby, but already making my brother's trademark expressions with her dark eyes.

The following morning, a Saturday, Michael decided to take me to the Bluewater shopping centre in Kent, an old favourite of ours. By the time we arrived, after over an hour driving on the motorway, added to all the previous day's travel, I had nasty cramps. I could not even walk. After five minutes there, we had to give up.

The results were ready a couple of weeks later. I had asked my mother to see Benigno herself, since she had known him for even longer than me. He had been her doctor at my youngest brother's birth over thirty years earlier. No confidentiality issues there. 'All was well with the foetus,' my mother told me jubilantly over the phone. I did not share her joy. If nothing wrong had been found with the foetus, my body had failed the baby.

THE BABY
An unexpected surprise

After my second miscarriage, my intuition – my gut feeling – was loud and clear. It was time to start investigations. I was somebody who had never had any health problems, a non-smoker, non-drinker, never used drugs, reasonably fit, with no previous miscarriages in my family or any other hereditary health issues. The 'you were unlucky' advice did not sound right to me.

The fact that we were being proactive as soon as we were back in London after my operation and looking into having a medical investigation kept me in high spirits. It was the 'doing something about it' that made me be positive. The best way to sort out a problem is by looking into finding solutions, not by sitting around, hoping next time we were going to be all right. I was convinced that the right doctor would give us some sought-after answers – once we found the *right doctor*. Travelling back and forth to Spain was going to be difficult – if cheaper – so we figured out we needed to find a miscarriage clinic in London.

Our first step was to find a doctor who could help us. I did not have a clue where to look for miscarriage medical advice. If someone has problems getting pregnant or needs IVF – and has the cash for it – there is quite a lot of help on offer; the underground in London is full of adverts about it. I could endure the grief of those couples who, like us, would do anything to have a baby. On the other hand, looking for a miscarriage specialist was not that easy. I decided to go to my GP as a starting point. That is what health advertisements always encourage you to do: consult your GP.

I contacted my surgery. Randomly, I was given an appointment with the senior doctor there. I was aware I needed to be 'unlucky' one more time to be able to go on the NHS. What I was after were directions on what type of doctor I should look for and the name of a good clinic or private hospital that could do a miscarriage investigation. This was not to do any tests on the foetus – that was being done in Spain at the time – but to research why this was happening by doing tests on myself and my partner, looking for clues into what was provoking the miscarriages and investigating whether something could be done to rectify it.

'I don't know of any,' came the short answer.

'Could you recommend any doctors we could talk to?' I persisted.

'No, I don't know of any.'

This was the same surgery where another doctor had shrugged his shoulders when I told him I was bleeding and I had requested an ultrasound scan. I came back home, disappointed once more but not defeated. There was always good old Google.

As it happened, that evening, after a quick online

search, I discovered that the best miscarriage clinic in Europe was at St Mary's Hospital in Paddington, where a Professor Lesley Regan was in charge. It was only a couple of miles from the surgery and my house. They would take private patients there.

It was December when I phoned Professor Regan's clinic. The earliest appointment they could give me was for August the following year. I could not see myself waiting for that long. I kept looking online and trying to find an earlier appointment. Eventually, I found an obstetrician at a private Wimbledon hospital, Mr Mackay, who listed miscarriage among his areas of expertise.

Many times since, I've wondered whether I should have made that appointment with Professor Regan and waited until August to meet her. Months later, when I saw a short television series presented by her, I was impressed. I bought a fantastic book written by her on pregnancy. I would have liked to learn whether Professor Regan had any ideas that could have helped us with other pregnancies. On the other hand, I got pregnant with my daughter six months before August. I guess there is no right answer.

Mr Isaac Mackay – second miscarriage investigation.

On my thirty-sixth birthday, to celebrate it in style, we had our first private meeting with Mr Mackay to investigate the reasons for my miscarriages. I crossed my fingers that my online search was going to pay off. I was so nervous, I left my favourite scarf behind in the taxi that took us to the hospital in Wimbledon. We had a comprehensive conversation with the consultant about our general health, family health, and previous pregnancy experiences, and nine tubes of blood were taken for tests.

Mr Mackay confirmed what we already knew: in other European countries, a second consecutive miscarriage will trigger an investigation; this is particularly relevant if the mother is of a certain age, since waiting for a third miscarriage may take away fertile time from her. This wasn't the case in England because of a lack of funds, not because medically it was necessarily the correct approach to take. Mr Mackay told us he was pushing hard for a change in the NHS; in his opinion, the reason it had not already happened was connected to the economic crisis the country was immersed in at the time.

We were encouraged by our meeting. During a dinner out to celebrate my birthday, we talked about what our steps would be. The best approach was to take it easy, avoid getting pregnant until we had some clear answers, and visit some relatives in Ireland whom Michael had not seen for years; then, at the end of it, when everything was settled, with a new magic pregnancy pill in our pocket, we would try again.

Tests for miscarriage.

Standard tests for miscarriage were the same everywhere we checked at the time.

Genetic testing: in about half of all early miscarriages, the baby does not develop normally right from the start and cannot survive. (Jumping ahead, that proved to be the case for me on two occasions.) Both of us were tested for abnormalities in our chromosomes (karyotyping). Nothing was found to be wrong. If genetic abnormalities had been the case for either of us, IVF would have been the right way to go, or even not having any children of our own.

Hormonal testing: women with irregular periods may find it harder to conceive, and when they do, they are more likely to miscarry. In my case, inconsistent periods were never a problem. This blood test checks the luteinising hormone to give you an idea of how generally fertile a woman is. My levels were sound and normal.

Immunological/blood clotting tests: problems with the blood vessels that feed the placenta can lead to miscarriage, particularly if the blood clots more than it should. This blood test needs to be done at least twice to avoid false positives and to pick up on anything that may not have shown up first time.

Measles: high body temperature can cause a miscarriage. After my first miscarriage, I went to the GP and received an MMR (measles, mumps, and rubella) jab. I didn't have the vaccination as a teenager, already a needle phobic; furthermore, I had been sure I didn't want to have babies. Rubella causes a milder illness than measles, but it is of particular concern because if a pregnant woman becomes infected, the virus can cause severe birth defects. An old friend of mine was born blind because her older brother got rubella when he was a baby and passed it on to their mum, who was pregnant with her. Birth defects resulting from congenital rubella can cause cataracts, glaucoma blindness, deafness, congenital heart defects, and intellectual disability in an unborn baby.

Ultrasound scans: these check the structure of the womb for any abnormalities. During my ultrasound scan, I was told I had a bicornuate uterus, which meant it was a heart shape instead of round. This could make a pregnancy more difficult and also make the baby breech since it would not be able to turn in the womb. There is nothing you can do to modify the shape of a bicornuate uterus; the left-hand side, which seemed to be a smaller cavity in my case, may not be large enough for the baby to grow. While it was safe for me to get pregnant, the main two issues were that the baby was almost certainly going to be breech and I would need a C-section.

I was rather surprised to learn about my bicornuate uterus, since I'd had over fifteen scans in Spain during my annual check-ups and it had never been mentioned to me that this was the case. I remembered being told during my first scan that my uterus dimensions were within the normal range, although towards the small size. If the shape was a reason for concern, I didn't understand why it hadn't been pointed out to me earlier. I called my mother that night to ask her to talk to Benigno next time she saw him to discuss this new information. I was out of my depth, confused by my lack of medical knowledge, and had no experience in the subject.

The strength of my cervix was also checked. A weak cervix may not be able to support the weight of a pregnancy and could cause a miscarriage, as happened to my friend Lola.

I had no fibroids. A fibroid is a growth of the muscle wall of the uterus and can cause a miscarriage if the egg tries to take hold onto it or near it, since it decreases the blood supply and the foetus cannot develop properly. Fibroids can be removed by surgery.

Over approximately two months, we went through all the recommended tests. We spent over £4,500 pounds. Nothing seemed to be obviously wrong. We had one last meeting with Mr Mackay, scheduled to discuss the results of a second set of blood tests and what to do next. There was no semen analysis because that was only done in cases where the woman could not get pregnant. As things went, before this last meeting, I was pregnant again.

Second chance for acupuncture.

Kylie, the acupuncturist I had previously visited, had been in my mind a lot, even though I had run away from her when she told me acupuncture could help with pregnancies. Pure science fiction. Yet, in the end, I had nothing to lose by trying. Acupuncture sounded ridiculous, but then I was going through a ludicrous situation with the miscarriages. Maybe the way to fight craziness was with more craziness.

Soon after my return from Spain, I booked an appointment to see Kylie. I told her about my second miscarriage, how much I wanted to have a baby, and my desire to get pregnant as soon as we had some answers from the miscarriage investigation that Mr Mackay was going to do. Kylie believed it was a good idea to prepare the body for the pregnancy. She maintained that acupuncture could target special points in my body to ensure it remained strong and resilient. She explained how acupuncture could improve my general health and get the body ready for all the stages of pregnancy, starting by getting the womb ready for fertilisation and producing a strong egg. Ideally, she said, we should do three to four months of sessions, targeting different pressure points depending on where I was in my monthly cycle.

What ultimately convinced me to give acupuncture a go was the fact that Kylie was contagiously enthusiastic and believed without a doubt in her work. Seeing somebody who was genuine, knowledgeable in her subject, and not afraid to take me on assured me I was doing the right thing.

I fell pregnant around three months into seeing her. Once I got pregnant, I saw her once a week without fail until week twelve. After that, I still saw her quite often – around every week until week twenty; then every two weeks, followed by once a month until the end of the pregnancy.

Discovering I was pregnant.

I got pregnant on a safe day, with the pregnancy monitor not showing a happy smiley on the display. The smiley did appear two days later. I started to feel hormonal, and a couple of days before my period was due, I bought a pregnancy test on my way to work. As soon as I reached my office floor, I ran for the loo. Positive. 'Impossible,' I said. I waited until lunchtime to go back to the pharmacy. I bought a different brand pregnancy test and hurried back to my office. Positive. I phoned Michael, elated, absolutely exultant. 'Impossible,' he said. 'We've been so careful.' Possible, and an early Valentine's Day present.

I went to see Kylie; we were still going through the pregnancy body preparation. I was not sure whether she was going to tell me off. The acupuncture sessions had been fine, with lots of needles on my lower tummy to redirect the energy towards my reproductive organs. Sometimes, I had a lot of pain on my belly afterwards, so we had to reduce the number of needles. Kylie was pleased about my pregnancy.

She told me not to worry about not having completed the full four months' preparation. She was always calm and positive. It was a joy to see her.

I did not go to see the GP. Nor did I contact Mr Mackay, since we had an appointment already arranged for a few days later. When we arrived for our meeting with Mr Mackay, we didn't give him time to speak; we blurted out the good news. He was pleased for us.

'I have some excellent news for you too,' he disclosed. He had found out why I had miscarried: on one – only one – of my blood tests, one of the three values related to an illness called antiphospholipid syndrome (APS) was positive – by a tiny amount. As a result of this illness, he explained, I needed to take a daily aspirin and have progesterone pessaries and an injection of heparin in my belly to make my blood thinner during my pregnancy.

I took the news badly. What did this illness mean in relation to my own health? I had never heard of it before. Did I have an autoimmune disease that could debilitate me and eventually kill me? If so, how come I had no idea about it? Certainly, I had spent half of my life taking ginseng so as not to be tired. I had once mentioned to a nurse, when registering with a new GP surgery, that I was always tired. She sharply replied: 'You live in London, you're working, you're also studying; of course you are tired – we're all tired in London!'

More importantly, no way could I inject myself every day. Above all, on my belly, when my instinct urged me to nurture and caress my belly, not stick needles in it. I asked whether the injection could be done somewhere else, on my arms or legs; anywhere else. Mr Mackay responded, 'No, the injections have to be done on the belly only.' I asked whether I could go somewhere else, to a private nurse or GP surgery, where they could do the injection for me, because there was no way I was capable of doing it. He said no, it was something that everybody was easily capable of doing by themselves. In the end, Michael agreed to do it.

The injection and aspirin were to make my blood thinner, making it easier for it to go through the placenta, so the foetus could get a healthy flow of blood. The doctor proceeded to show Michael how to inject me. I got terribly stabbed in my belly. It hurt awfully and itched madly for a long time. I got my first bruise the size of a fist. And I had five months of it ahead of me.

When my diabetic grandfather got Parkinson's disease, he was not able to inject himself, so my grandmother had to do it for him. She had no idea how to do it. Scared, she would close her eyes and stab him hard with the needle to make sure it went in the first time. He took it well, with just a kind, 'Victoria, one day you are going to kill me.' Michael took much the same approach.

On all my blood tests, I had a low Protein-S reading. I asked about this issue, but it did not seem to be relevant. It was lucky I did not learn about all the potential complications and treatments until I was already pregnant. Otherwise, I might have decided not to have my own children.

I asked to be signed off work for three weeks, until the end of week eight. I didn't want to move at all or even leave the house. I could not risk another failure. 'Put your feet up when you next get pregnant,' was the advice of the older women amongst my family and friends, including Erika, Michael's mum, who herself had suffered several miscarriages. When she'd got pregnant with Michael, she had lain on a sofa for nine months.

Mr Mackay was reluctant; he guaranteed there was no reason for anything to go wrong now that we were certain of the cause of my two previous miscarriages: 'You will be more than fine with the right medical treatment. You should lead a normal life.' Ultimately, he signed me off to keep me calm but not because he believed it was a clinical necessity.

We left the hospital with the injections and the progesterone. The aspirin, we were told, we could buy it at any pharmacy. We were advised to stop all consumption of caffeine and to avoid getting a cold or fever. I do not drink coffee or tea, but I keep awake with Diet Coke and need one or two a day to function normally. That was a serious blow.

We went home, where I did some online research on antiphospholipid syndrome. The illness in itself looked threatening, certainly a life-changing condition. While I did not think I fitted the profile, I was fearful for my health and future. A common problem for people with antiphospholipid syndrome is high blood pressure, which is dangerous for any person, and even more so for pregnant women, because they may end up suffering from pre-eclampsia, which is a life-threatening problem when pregnant. However, I have always had a problem with low blood pressure. I have fainted several times in my life. I was once responsible for the morning delay on the Jubilee Line in London. Several members of both my mother and father's families suffer from low blood pressure and occasional faintness – all simply sorted with caffeine or a salty snack. I tried to discuss this with Michael and Mr Mackay during other appointments, but my research was quickly dismissed. In any case, there was no other treatment for miscarriage: 'It is this or nothing', I was told.

The next morning, I went to the GP to let them know about my pregnancy. Afterwards, I walked to Sainsbury's to buy the aspirin I needed. The pharmacist asked me why I needed to buy it, but when I told her I was pregnant and had APS, she refused to sell it to me. I explained my recently diagnosed health issues and previous failed pregnancies. I told her that I had been advised to take it by an expert doctor in difficult pregnancies and that I had discussed it with the GP that very same morning. She still refused to sell it to me. I grew very frustrated. She told me I was confused or misinformed, because 'pregnant women are not allowed aspirin'. Nothing I explained worked. As usual, I sent *the man* on his way back home from work. He spoke to the store manager and the pharmacist, got the aspirins, an apology, and a £30 store card for all the trouble. I find these experiences extremely frustrating: is a woman's knowledge not to be trusted?

I stayed at home for three weeks, most of the time in bed. I was scared of moving. After Mr Mackay's recommendation to reduce caffeine, I stopped drinking Diet Coke and took all my medicines every day, which included blood pressure reducers. From the moment I woke up, faint and dizzy, my day was monotonous. Sometimes, I could not get up from bed and spent the whole day lying down without eating, because going downstairs to the kitchen was far too much of an effort. I didn't know whether that was a normal pregnancy symptom or whether I was so scared I was imagining symptoms or making myself ill with worry. I wondered how other women coped if they had to go to work or if they had other older children in the house.

I told Erika, my mother-in-law, about this. She said that was not normal at all; it was one thing to be a bit tired, but what I was describing was not right. She added that I should check my blood pressure, so Michael bought a monitor. The reading was dangerously low.

I called my uncle, the pharmacist, to ask him what to do. I went back on the Diet Coke, olives, and crisps, all with the intention of raising my blood pressure. My body perked up straightaway. My levels of energy went back to almost normal. It was a relief to learn that pregnancies do not have to be that bad.

I was still seeing Kylie once a week and went for a private scan every week for the next month. We saw the tiny embryo at the two weeks' scan. At the next scan, we marvelled at the three millimetre foetus with its tiny brain and heart. I told Michael that it looked like him already. We heard the galloping heartbeat in week eight. Wonderful.

Wisdom recommends that couples don't announce a pregnancy until week twelve; in our case, we had shared the good news with everybody at work because of my time off and with everyone in the family because they were concerned about our previous experiences.

Once we were in week eight and there was a healthy heartbeat, Mr Mackay told us we were more than safe. We should lead a normal life like any other pregnant couple. Now that I was on the treatment, the pregnancy was risk-free. He did not share my worries.

We were going to drive to Dublin for St Patrick's Day, not fly – which in theory could be a bit riskier for the pregnancy. I was keen on Michael reconnecting with his dad's family in Ireland, with lots of cousins, aunts, and uncles and many other distant relatives that he did not get to see often. I was excited too. The idea of a normal pregnancy and being able to enjoy my blossoming was fabulous. Nonetheless, my idea was to keep it simple: better be safe and slow down for the next few months.

We drove on a Sunday all the way to Wales, about four to five hours' drive caused by the usual traffic jams trying to get out of London. We took a friend and his daughter in the car with us, who were going back to Dublin after a London trip. There was lots of advice on what to do in Dublin and conversations about life with his four children. I found the long trip more difficult that I had expected. In Holyhead, we caught the ferry to Dublin. It was a rough crossing, not that uncommon on those waters. At times, it was even impossible to stand up. Michael's dad, who had taken the ferry to and fro for years, had a little story about dancing to keep calm when the sea was choppy. He used to get amusing looks from crew and passengers. I didn't dance but grabbed the arms of my seat as if my life depended on it and looked forward to having firm soil under my feet. By the time we arrived at the hotel, it was quite late, and I was tired and shaken.

The next morning, we went to see the St Patrick's Day parade. It was sunny but freezing cold. After a couple of hours walking around, I started to feel unwell, tired, cold, and dizzy. I told Michael I needed to sit down, so we looked for a place to have lunch. I was falling asleep over my food. Sitting was uncomfortable, and I wanted to lay down. We took a cab back to the hotel, where I had to go to bed. By now I was feeling feverish. Mr Mackay had told us how important it was not to have a fever in the early stages on the pregnancy. I lay on the bed, hot and sleepy.

Michael did not want to stay all afternoon in the hotel. We were meant to call his family to arrange when to meet up. I was spoiling the holiday, I knew, but I was not up for it. Michael decided to go out for a walk, maybe reasoning that I was a hormonal nervous pregnant woman. He had been told a few times how nutty pregnant women can get. As far as he was concerned, if Mr Mackay had said I was fine, then I was fine.

I didn't mind him going out and fell asleep soon after he left. After about five hours, I woke up and went to the toilet: blood. For about one hour, the blood kept coming. I feared the worst. I didn't know what to do. By then, I knew that if a miscarriage had started, there was nothing I could do to stop it; rushing to a hospital in Dublin – wherever the hospital was in Dublin – was not going to stop the bleeding. I had read enough about antiphospholipid syndrome in the last few weeks to believe that could not be my problem either. I had a chill sense of despair.

I missed Kylie. She had told me that if I ever felt unwell, I should see her straightaway. But there was a rough sea between the two of us.

When Michael came back, he couldn't understand how it could be happening again. He insisted I had to have the injection to make my blood thinner, though I certainly didn't want to have it. At that stage, I didn't think my blood needed to be any thinner and believed it was wrong to give blood thinners to a bleeding person. I fell asleep again, my feverish body having no energy to keep going or argue.

I slept soundly all night, but the next morning, the bed looked like a battlefield: blood everywhere. It was like a horror movie set. It was all over my clothes, my arms, hands, even my face, the bed, the pillow, the duvet.

I went to the toilet, dreading to look inside my knickers.

I wanted to be by myself – me and my baby. I was not sure what I was going to find there. I looked at my blood-smeared face, bloody hands, and bloody pyjamas in the bathroom mirror. I got ready to look inside my clothes.

Blood everywhere, but not a spot on my underwear. My knickers were as clean as new. That did not make any sense at all. *How did I manage to get not only myself but the whole bed all messy with blood? Where was it coming from?*

I went back to the room and tried to mimic my possible movements in bed during the night. The blood had in fact come from the hole in my belly where I had been injected the night before. It was a hole large enough to be easy visible to the naked eye. My belly and back were covered in red.

We cancelled our holiday and drove back home, with me lying flat in the car for the whole journey. I managed to get an appointment with Kylie instantly. She assured me I was going to be fine and knew what points to target on my body. I closed my eyes while lying on the treatment bed. I calmed down, safe with her.

Mr Mackay was on holiday. It took us five long days to have an ultrasound scan at his clinic. When we had our appointment, it was confirmed that a miscarriage had started and stopped – the scan showed the 'dark circles' surrounding the embryo area. The image also revealed the best news ever: the baby was still alive.

It was the first time we saw our baby looking like a baby. I was ten weeks pregnant. We could see a head, a body, arms, legs, although still not feet or arms. It was wriggling a lot. It was genuinely overwhelming, seeing our baby.

I wanted to discuss the treatment again. The possible reasons for the bleeding, how to keep the pregnancy going. We told Mr Mackay what had happened and that I did not agree with his diagnosis. He found no explanation for the bleeding from the belly. He assumed I was exaggerating: 'Women and blood!' He maintained I needed to follow his treatment for the whole nine months of the pregnancy. I wanted a second opinion, but the truth was, we had not found anybody else to talk to.

My baby was alive. It was the best possible news. There were unanswered questions: the medical treatment, that I did not judge I needed in the first place, had not stopped the bleeding. Was the baby alive thanks to the acupuncture, dismissed by the doctors as science fiction? How could I be sure my baby was going to be safe for the rest of the pregnancy?

When we left hospital, Michael told me, 'You are totally amazing because you can create life.' A beautiful and stone-heavy compliment all in one. I was proud but nervous. There is such a thin line between success and failure.

Choosing a hospital

It was nearly week twelve in the pregnancy when the time came for me to choose a maternity hospital. I did my homework after my two bad experiences at St George's. A caring man, Mr Mackay was keen on me choosing St George's, because he worked there too on the NHS and he wanted to keep an eye on us. However, I told him there was no chance of me choosing that hospital and explained that I regarded the medical care we had received there in my previous pregnancies to have been below standard.

He was disappointed but said he could understand my reasons. While I know it is unfair to dismiss everybody who works in a hospital, a person should not take risks with their health. For me, it is better to minimise the risks. At the end of the day, I would not go back to a restaurant if I'd had food poisoning there once or to a hotel that was not up to standards even if I had only been there once.

I checked the rating lists of maternity wards provided by the Care Quality Commission. I understand this list is no longer publicly available since the hospitals at the bottom of it were not pleased about it. This is the wrong approach in my humble opinion. If I want to choose a school or a university, buy a house, work for a company with good environmental practices, and so forth, there are rankings and rates for categorically everything. It is for customers to choose to read or ignore them, to believe or to question them, and hiding information never looks good.

I was allowed to choose between the five hospitals in our borough: the two geographically nearest to us were the old Mayday in Croydon (now renamed Croydon University

Hospital) and St George's, which both happened to be at the bottom of the list in England. I was lucky I was entitled to choose St Thomas', also in Lambeth, which was towards the top of the list and had good reviews for high-risk pregnancies. When discussing it with my local GP, he tried to dissuade me from St Thomas'. 'They are far too busy there,' he claimed, 'since everybody wants to be there. It's better to choose a different hospital. You get great care in all hospitals anyway.' I went for St Thomas' all the same. It was also the nearest hospital to my office. Since the pregnancy appointments were only available during my working hours, St Thomas was the most convenient location, being the nearest hospital to my office and easier to reach by public transport.

The midwives

I was on a high when I went for my first meeting with the midwives at St Thomas'. I had made it to the safe side.

There were two teams of midwives at St Thomas'. Since my pregnancy was considered high risk, I was assigned to the Thames midwives, who were in charge of difficult pregnancies. This includes women with histories ranging from previous miscarriages to heart problems, diabetes, and so forth. I was going to meet with two sets of doctors too, one for my antiphospholipid problem and a further team of general obstetricians.

During my first meeting with a Thames midwife, she

told me each time I had an appointment that I was going to meet a different midwife, which was done to ensure I would be looked after during the birth by somebody I had already met. My meetings were always going to be on a Monday afternoon, because that was the allocated day for women with APS problems. I was given a yellow book, my maternity notebook, for all the notes concerning my pregnancy, hospital visits, and birth plan. Each time I had an appointment, the staff, doctors, and midwives had to write in it the details of any discussions, issues, and progress of the pregnancy. The book had a sticker on the cover with a telephone number in case, at any time, twenty-four seven, I had a problem, a question, or was not feeling well. It was a direct line to the Thames midwives. It felt a refreshing to be there.

During the same week, I had my week twelve scan. All was confirmed to be well with the baby. Good development, regular size, vigorous heartbeat, no Down's syndrome, or chromosome 13, or chromosome 18 abnormalities.

When I first met the APS doctor at St Thomas', I had to retake all the blood tests I had taken privately, although I showed her copies of the earlier results. When I saw her at the next appointment, she told me the tests were negative; there was no evidence I had APS. I was in week fourteen of my pregnancy. The doctor told me I should stop the medication for two reasons: firstly, there was no evidence I needed it in the first place; secondly, because even for women with APS, they stop the medication in week twelve. No more injections, no more progesterone. I was told to keep going with the aspirin until the end of the pregnancy.

I was told that, for future pregnancies, APS or no APS, I should do what I had done for this pregnancy since it had worked. By this point, everybody presumed the pregnancy was safe. It seemed about as scientific an approach as when I took my lucky pen to exams as a child or my friend's lucky football underpants. I believe a patient needs to understand the reasons behind a treatment in order to agree with it, not to have it imposed on them. It was not clear why I should have the treatment in future pregnancies if the conclusion was that I hadn't needed it in the first place. However, it was time to concentrate on the current pregnancy and forget about the rest. One pregnancy at a time.

I asked the doctor whether I could do the injections in another part of my body in a future hypothetical pregnancy, rather than my belly, which by then looked like a punch bag. She replied it was unequivocally safe to do them on the arms or legs. It was just a matter of personal preference.

I met Michael for a pub dinner to celebrate the good news. I was over the moon; my constant companions, little Miss Fears and Mr Worries, were packed and gone. My life could go back to normal. My body felt safe for the first time in almost two years. That evening, I had my one and only alcoholic drink for the rest of the pregnancy and beyond: a classic mojito.

I got into a routine with the hospital. The APS doctor

had told me she didn't need to see me again because I had no APS. However, I still needed to keep my appointments on Mondays because that was my allocated slot. I was going to have regular meetings with the midwives and the obstetrician team. Non-risk pregnancies do not get to see the obstetricians, only a team of midwives allocated to non-risk pregnancies.

Hospital appointments were always during working hours, and I had more of them than a regular pregnant woman. As a public sector worker, I was allowed to attend them without having to take holiday time or do extra hours of work. Just the half smiles from my boss: 'Hospital appointment again?' Despite my boss, I realised how lucky I was. I could attend them without fear of work repercussions or being sacked. Many times I have this reported in the news.

The appointments, though, were tiresome. An average of two hours' waiting was the norm to see both doctors and midwives. There was an enormous waiting room in one of the top floors of the building. It was hot, being high up in a glass building with no apparent air conditioning. Mondays were the busiest day, the staff always said – it was like shopping in Oxford Street in London on a busy Saturday afternoon. You couldn't squeeze in one more pregnant woman.

A few of us got talking once. I noticed every time the doctor's door opened, we all started to get up from our seats, hoping somebody was going to shout out our name. When chatting, we discovered we all had an appointment with the same doctor for two o'clock: no wonder the waiting area was busy.

At the end of each appointment, we had to take our yellow book to the main reception area to book a new appointment according to the instructions written down by the midwife or doctor. On one occasion, the receptionist told me if it was okay for me to have the next midwife appointment on a Wednesday morning because they were literary empty then and Mondays were far too busy. Sounded good to me.

When I arrived, it was wonderful. An empty waiting room. Only me. The midwife I saw – who also worked there on Mondays – was grumpy. She told me I shouldn't be there because Wednesday morning was the day for diabetic pregnant women. What a fuss, since there were no diabetic pregnant women needing attention or, in fact, any other pregnant women waiting to be seen.

In the early stages of pregnancy, I had two serious concerns, but I was getting no answers: toxoplasmosis and group B streptococcus screening. I asked about this and tried to discuss it with the midwifes.

Toxoplasmosis and group B streptococcus screening

Toxoplasmosis is an infection caused by a parasite in the meat of infected animals and the faeces of infected cats. Most adults can deal with the infection comfortably. More worryingly, in pregnant women, it can cause miscarriage and stillbirth.

In Spain, there is a standard free test for every pregnant woman, since traditionally, the Spanish eat lots of ham and pig products. When I first arrived in England, it was quite difficult to find serrano ham and chorizo, but these days you can buy them anywhere. It looks like there is a successful market for them. Nevertheless, the midwives told me there was no test for it on the NHS since nobody here eats cured meats – or have cats, I guess. I asked whether I could have the test done somewhere privately. They didn't know about private clinics, so I stopped eating cured meats to be on the safe side. Easier said than done. And I still had the cat in the house.

I also asked about group B streptococcus screening because I have a good English friend in London, who is a GP, whose first baby died during birth because of this infection. In Spain, there is another standard free test for it, as 25 per cent of women carry these bacteria. A woman may not know about it because it does not affect her health; however, during a vaginal birth, these bacteria can make a child acutely unwell from diseases, including meningitis; in some extreme cases, it may cause stillbirth.

If a woman is tested and gets a positive result, the only thing she will need to do is take antibiotics during a vaginal birth. One of my sisters-in-law had a positive result when tested and was given antibiotics when she went into labour. Her baby was fine, but what if she had not been tested? I may not have a goddaughter now.

Lots has been written in the news about it, sadly, invariably prompted by couples who have lost their babies. The test costs £15.

If it was a matter of cost, I do not understand why I was force to have blood test to check my blood group every time I went to the same hospital with a new pregnancy or because I needed a procedure related to the pregnancy. That costs money. There was no need for that blood test; my blood type was written in my hospital records and on their computer system. 'You have tested me more than five times,' I used to tell them, 'and it is AB+ – it doesn't change.' 'Yes, we know, it is on our system,' they would reply, 'but the NHS rules state we have to test you again.'

As all pregnant women are, I was routinely tested for HIV and MRSA. I was told by a midwife that some women do not know they are HIV positive, and this test would protect the midwives from getting infected. I was sure I didn't have HIV, but I didn't know whether I had bacteria that could possibly kill my baby. Shouldn't we also be trying to protect unborn children?

Even if hospitals cannot afford the routine strep test, I believed women should be informed of the risks. Maybe they could pay for the test by themselves if they can afford it or have it for free if they can't. I cannot imagine anybody opting out for a £15 test that could save the life of her child.

Heartbeat monitor

Around week sixteen of my pregnancy, the midwives started to use a foetal heartbeat monitor to listen to the baby's heartbeat during my appointments. As soon as I saw the device, I decided to buy my own and bought the same baby foetal Doppler heart monitor. We had already tried a different type of prenatal heart monitor advertised in all the baby magazines. It was much cheaper, but I wasn't sure about it. It was designed as a belt that the woman places around her belly. While I could hear some cavernous noises when using it, those indeterminate sounds could have been intergalactic rumblings or, who knows, even my dinner being digested. I had stopped using it because I didn't think it was worth it.

This new monitor was fantastic, although it was five times more expensive, plus I had to buy ultrasound gel to spread on my tummy. For me, the peace of mind made the expense worthwhile. The device was uncomplicated to use, and there was no chance of mistaking my heartbeat for the baby's. A foetus' heartbeat is much faster than an adult heartbeat. In my case, my heartbeat is less than 70 bpm, and the foetus was around 200 bpm. I spread out some ultrasound gel over my tummy before moving the stick around – the smaller the baby, the more I needed to move it until I started hearing the heartbeat.

I listened to my baby's heartbeat every single day but limited myself to doing it 'only' three times a day. It was beautiful and calming. It was what I needed. I couldn't wait for days or weeks until my next hospital visit or private scan to hear it.

Have a break, have a scan

There are two ultrasound scans on the NHS: week twelve to confirm the pregnancy and check for any abnormalities and week twenty to check all the baby's organs are developing properly and whether the sex of the baby can be found out.

We had extra, private scans for reassurance at a cost of about £200 per scan. Expensive, but then again, for me, it was a lifesaver – my own life in this case – and the reassurance let me get on with enjoying the moment and trying to live normally.

In week seventeen, we went to a clinic on Harley Street. There were a few ultrasound scan options depending on the reason for the scan. We wanted a plain reassurance scan. There was a 'find out the sex of the baby' scan on offer, but that was from week twenty.

The technician told us – without us asking – that if the sex of the baby was clear to her, she could tell us if we paid an extra £35. That was exciting. After confirming all was well with the pregnancy, she told us she could see the sex of the baby without a doubt.

'Are you ready?'

'Of course, we are.'

'It's a girl.'

All of a sudden, my baby had a face; a girl's face. I could give her a name.

We left the clinic £235 poorer, but my goodness, we were overjoyed. I called my family in Spain straightaway. 'It is a girl, a healthy girl!'

That clinic is now a London landmark for us. If we are nearby, we walk by it and cherish the memories of the exciting news we received on our first visit there.

Three weeks later, I went for my week twenty scan at St Thomas', where a kind Australian technician was excited to tell me the sex of the baby. I told him I knew she was a girl and the reason why I knew it, which spoiled his surprise. I should have kept my secret. He confirmed she was a girl. All was still well with the pregnancy.

At this point, I started to notice the baby move continually. In hospital, we were told I needed to feel the baby moving ten times a day – if it was less than that I should call them because it could be a sign that something was not right. My baby never stopped moving. I never counted the times I enjoyed experiencing the sensation.

All her little habits and personality started to make themselves known to us. Active day and night, except for a few hours during the morning, between breakfast and lunch, when she always took it easy – and does even now. She had a total dislike of being on trains and loud noises – we had to abandon a Bruce Springsteen concert, she was obviously not a fan – and as a little girl, she moans on trains, and we have to change carriages if a loud school group gets on ours.

Before she was born, I used to caress her head through my belly to put her to sleep and play music to calm her down if she was bored when we were still in the office in the afternoon. If I got annoyed, she instantly got annoyed. She is still the same girl.

She was getting bigger too. After a week of wondering why I had a constant stitch in my right-hand side – when all I did was walk sluggishly – I put my hands on my waist and felt something like a hard football there. After some further touching, I realised it was the baby's head.

I never got a kick from her. She was into stretching, head pushing up and out of the top right-hand side of my belly, pressing against my ribs, feet pushing down at the bottom of my belly and hands pushing forward near my belly button, all at the same time. After she was born, I regularly saw her doing the same action in her cot. It made me smile, my little Pilates girl.

I booked a pregnancy massage appointment at the Zita West Fertility Clinic. I had heard so much about them, I wanted to have a peek at their centre. They also deal with miscarriage; some of the doctors there also worked at St Mary's and looked very good, albeit expensive. When mentioning Zita West to those in the NHS – and the extra number of tests they do there – the reply was those tests don't prove any factual reasons for miscarriage. It was more about general wellbeing, health, and being calm. However, we should all care more about our general happiness, pregnancy or no pregnancy.

The smokers in the family

All was going surprisingly well. I travelled to Spain by myself for a week in the summer, where I had a massive argument with some members of my family because they wanted to smoke in front of me while we were having lunch at a restaurant. I was told, 'You're intolerant, you have no respect for smokers!' Sadly, two of them are now suffering from cancer, and we are all suffering with them.

While in Spain, I went to see Benigno. I had a scan and we saw the baby in a breech position. I mentioned the midwives said it was possible to turn breech babies. He disagreed with this. It was a dangerous practice that had been stopped in Spain over ten years earlier. It can seriously damage the baby and the mother. The odds are it will not work, and, in some cases, it could trigger an emergency C-section. I told him the advice of the College of Obstetricians in England was exactly what he had said, and it was unclear to me why the midwives were so keen on doing it. I also asked him for his opinion on my blood results, and he too didn't think I had APS. However, he thought the constant low Protein S could be more of an issue, although there was not enough research at the time into how it could affect pregnancy.

Students in charge

Back in London, I continued with my work and hospital routine. Now, I am always up for helping students. Education is the best gift a person can receive. In my dealings with hospitals, I always agreed to a medical student being present and to answering students' questions or helping in any way I could. I had an A-level student doing office work experience with me at the time, and I loved having him there and giving him 'real' work to do.

However, when a nursing student was left unsupervised and in charge of taking blood samples from all the pregnant women at the hospital, she managed to contaminate every single one. When she had to phone each of us to apologise and ask us to come back for a new blood test, I was not impressed.

Another time, I was left with a medical student who looked like he didn't want to end up in obstetrics. He didn't manage to make sense of the heart monitor. 'It doesn't work,' he announced. Luckily, I had been using my monitor at home before the appointment and was pretty confident that things were all right. He told me I needed to go back on the medication that I had stopped taking over ten weeks earlier at the advice of the senior doctors – back on injections, back on progesterone – and afterwards put his hands on my belly for less than a second, then quickly reported that my baby was 'perfect'. Thank you. I told him everything he was suggesting was in disagreement with his senior doctor and that he needed to double-check his advice. He left me waiting outside for thirty minutes, while my heart rate went through the roof. Consequently, the baby, sensing my nervousness, started jumping up and down distressingly. He came back to tell me to follow the advice of the senior doctor and to forget what he had said. We were done for the day.

Despite this sort of incident, Michael and I were enjoying the pregnancy as a couple. When I was over seven months pregnant, we went to a local photographer for a photo shoot of us plus the huge belly. We settled on a name, Victoria, after my grandmother. We even dared to go on a short holiday and flew to Vienna. We started buying things for our baby and decorating her nursery, which used to be an empty room and Treacle's favourite hangout. In fact, we used to call it Treacle's room. Treacle was not impressed; she didn't want the hassle.

Breech babies

It was über uncomfortable when the midwives squeezed my belly to check the position of the baby. The baby disliked it too and tried to move away, as one midwife told me. On account of all my private scans, I knew the baby was breech. I also knew she could not turn because of the shape of my uterus and because I could touch her head and outstretched feet and hands several times each day.

Nevertheless, the midwives kept saying they weren't

sure the baby was breech: 'It could be the bottom and not the head.' I repeatedly told them it was the head at the top, because it was round, big, and rock hard; what's more, I could sense her feet at the bottom of my belly and her hands pushing on my belly button. I had also seen it in scans, in some cases only twenty-four hours earlier, and had the scan prints with me to prove it. Once, I got into an argument, since, after having the conversation about the baby's position, the midwife went ahead and drew a picture in my yellow book that showed the baby head down, bottom up, legs and arms facing my back. I crossed it out. The argument continued at the next appointment when I had to make it clear again why I was angry and frustrated. Afterwards, they apologised.

When I was nearly eight months pregnant, another highly trained specialist midwife – no more than twenty-five years old – told me that before trying for a C-section, they were going to try to turn the baby, as this was the standard procedure. She informed me there was a risk it could break my waters or damage the baby; in which case, an emergency C-section would be performed, which was why this procedure was always carried out next to an emergency theatre. I told her that the Royal College of Obstetricians recommends never trying to move a breech baby in a bicornuate uterus because of all the risks to the baby and the mother. The decision should be taken by an obstetrician, not a midwife. That sort of appointment made me panic.

At work, my boss and I interviewed candidates for my

maternity cover. I was ready to stop working when I was eight months pregnant. I was enormous; walking anywhere took me double the time it used to. I enjoyed rubbing my belly in circles. Victoria was large, and it was easy to distinguish the different parts of her body. Once, she stretched out her hand with such strength that I could touch her five fingers. At night, she kept trying to butt her head out, pushing up against my ribs. I rubbed her head gently until she fell asleep.

Last month of pregnancy and pee madness

During my last month of pregnancy, I kept waking up at night, almost every hour, to go for a pee. It's a common nightmare for pregnant women and everybody living with them. Getting up for a toilet trip is not a quick excursion when you have a humongous belly: first trying to get up from bed, invariably waking up baby, who is always keen to join the party, going back to bed, trying to lie back, positioning my belly on one side, but the baby not liking the new position, having to rearrange myself once more. After her rearrangement, I needed some rearrangement too. A few grunts from the man in the bed. Everybody settled. Sixty minutes later, let's do it all again.

When my sister-in-law was pregnant, my brother slept in a different room for the final weeks of the pregnancy. He persuaded himself it would be helpful if at least one of them slept through the night. Charming.

Other than the endless pee trips, I didn't suffer from any other common pregnancy problems: no constipation, no morning sickness or any other time of the day sickness, no dizziness, no tired legs, no haemorrhoids, no stretch marks, no indigestion, and so forth. Only the fear that anything could go wrong at any time. Maybe that was why I found many of my midwife appointments pointless, as I had no issues they could deal with.

Pregnancy propaganda

The hospital was adamant about us attending two appointments as a couple: one about breastfeeding and one about the amazing experience of giving birth vaginally. Michael didn't want to go. I didn't want to go either, but as we were first-time future parents, the hospital insisted on us attending.

I came out angry from both. It was like watching a scary movie where I had been kidnapped by a brainwashing sect. They insisted on pushing their agenda rather than having a discussion. We were forced to take part in a forum where women's different opinions were not respected and where we were endlessly patronised. It was not surprising that we were all first-time parents there; you do not go back for a second round willingly. There was not two-way dialogue, no respect for different opinions or women's preferences. We are not all the same. Natural birth without pain relief forced on every woman is not right.

Their message was clear: breastfeeding is super easy. Put the baby on your nipple. Breastfeeding works as production on demand; mums with big babies will produce more milk than mums with small babies who don't need to feed that much. Women who breastfeed lose the pregnancy weight much faster, and more importantly, it will protect the woman from breast cancer. Breastfed babies do not get colic and have no allergies as children or adults; they will perform better in life, with good brains and successful careers. It was better than winning the lottery.

However, what about those women who don't want to breastfeed? And what about women who cannot breastfeed? What about when babies need more milk? I know cases when it hasn't worked; for instance, my grandmother could not be breastfed because her own mother got pregnant with her sister when she was only two months old (and my grandmother lived healthily and happily until the young age of ninety-four). My own mother was told by the doctor to combine breastfeeding with formula milk because my big brothers needed it. And what about leaving the baby with grandparents? What about the dad helping out with feeding the baby in the middle of the night? What about the mothers who need medication and can't breastfeed? There was no room for discussion. Breastfeeding full-time for a year was the only answer. In 2019, BBC *Woman's Hour* dedicated a full week to the topic of breastfeeding and the different experiences that women go through. Some of them were pretty hard to listen to.

The midwife giving the talk told us she had only breastfed her baby for a year, and the baby kept crying. 'She was just a naughty baby,' she told us. 'Some babies cry all the time.' Somebody dared to ask: 'Maybe the baby was hungry? Did you check with somebody else?' No, came the reply: no need to check. Breastfeeding is the best and must not be complemented; it's more than enough food for the baby for the first year of life.

I left feeling uneasy. I was being talked to as if I were a three-year-old. It could not be that clean cut: you breastfeed, you don't get breast cancer; you don't breastfeed, you are damned. What about respecting women's lives, opinions, and feelings? In any case, I decided I wanted to breastfeed; I was more than ready for it.

The second meeting I found rather upsetting as well. It was about giving birth the good old way: no painkillers and vaginal delivery. The only good way, apparently. The day started with a video of a woman delivering a baby the good way. It was gory, with a constant soundtrack of screaming. The perfect Halloween movie.

The whole day was about experiencing the pain during birth and your poop coming out, because motherhood is about suffering, and a painful birth is the first step on the long path of wearisome motherhood.

There was no room to discuss women's preferences

or opinions. 'Of course, if a woman needs painkillers, she should have them,' we were told. 'However, it is better not to start with them.' Most couples there had heard of this trick. First, it is too early for painkillers. Then they cannot find the anaesthetist for an epidural, and finally, it is too late for an epidural to work, according to the midwives. Several of my friends went through this process; they learnt their lesson the hard way. They were better prepared for the second birth: ask for the painkillers as soon as you arrive, be assertive, speak up.

As part of our talk, we were taken to visit the delivery section of the hospital. There was a big reception area, with lots of couples waiting to be allocated somewhere to have their baby. There was an enormous double door at the end of the reception area that gave access to the birth area. Every few minutes, the double doors would open and a woman would appear, either in a wheelchair or a bed, with a little baby in her arms. Every single person around the reception area, especially the pregnant women arriving to give birth, and their partners would stare at these women in awe. I called it 'the little walk of fame'.

We were told about vaginal tearing. It is better to let it tear naturally, was the advice. That way, it only tears as much as it needs to do. We were shown the large, thick, curved needle that the midwives used to stitch the tear. No need for a painkiller for the stitches. The woman is in so much pain from everything else that she won't notice, our smiling speaker told us. This is not a I know better than you discussion on vaginal tearing, but the advice in Spain is the exact opposite: the chances of not naturally tearing are close to none, and letting the body tear naturally will result in a zigzag cut that is more difficult to sew and heal. More importantly, an obstetrician, who is always present during birth, whether it is a high-risk or low-risk pregnancy, will do the cut, under anaesthetic, to give a better chance of recovery for the pregnant woman. A midwife will attend the birth as a helper.

It is a woman's choice. Right choices come from the right information.

Some friends of mine were flying back to their countries of origin to give birth and needed a doctor's letter to be allowed to fly when heavily pregnant. I didn't consider it. I didn't want to risk flying. I wanted to be with Michael and at home after the birth, rather than waiting in Spain for six to eight weeks to return.

By the time we finished the talk, I was clearer than ever that, for medical reasons – or simply because I had decided it was my choice and I would pay for it if necessary – I was having a C-section.

C-section confirmation

In September, I caught a cold I could not get rid of. I was getting no rest at night between the bouts of coughing and the constant getting up to go to the toilet. The cough, persistent and strong, made my belly shake up and down.

The pain ran down from my throat to my chest, down to my belly every time I coughed. In the end, I decided to try my luck and see the GP. I knew he could give me antibiotics because they do not affect the baby. But no chance. He refused to give me any medication for the cough, which continued to get worse. One Saturday at the end of September, after hours of coughing, I got up to go to the loo. I flushed without looking, then decided to wipe a second time because instinct told me something was wrong. There was blood on the toilet paper. Not much, but enough to turn my world upside down.

I ran to our room and woke up Michael. We drove to hospital in the middle of the night, panicking, in total silence. The baby, always active, was quiet. We arrived within fifteen minutes and were sent to the delivery section of the maternity ward. I was asked first to check whether there was more blood. None. We went to sit down in the waiting room. Mercifully, the baby decided to wake up and start wriggling. She was alive.

I was connected to a baby heart monitor and left on a bed to rest. Everybody kept asking me how much blood had come out when I went to the loo. 'Was it as much as a tea spoon? A large spoon? Two spoons?' I wasn't sure, since I had done the whole loo thing in the dark and I hadn't anticipated a problem at this late stage of the pregnancy. I told everybody I hoped the reason for it was my relentless cough rather than pregnancy problems. The baby's heartbeat was fine, my cervix was closed – aka not preparing for delivery. I had an ultrasound scan, and the technician told us there was a lot of amniotic liquid, which could be a sign that the baby had started to pee, because it was a big baby, virtually ready to come out – therefore nothing to worry about. Or it could be a worrying sign of polyhydramnios, which indicated a problem with the baby's health and development.

By early morning, the hospital advised us to go home and rest. I had an appointment scheduled on the following Monday to see the obstetrician to talk about the current developments and the birth plan. We were on edge – we were close to a happy ending and at the same time so close to a catastrophic end. I asked Michael to come to the doctor with me. We needed to present our case strongly; we could not lose the baby now.

This was the first and last time we met Dr Bewley, the doctor in charge of the high-risk pregnancies at St Thomas' at the time. Thankfully, it was not with another of her students; we were not in the mood for it. We explained, calmly, clearly, what had happened at the weekend, my two miscarriages, the problems with this pregnancy, and my bicornuate uterus. We reminded her that the baby was breech and stated that we wanted a C-section arranged. She answered "Yes" within a second.

She told us that the advice given by the midwife about trying to turn the baby was incorrect. Then Dr Bewley told us she was concerned for us both – Michael and I – because we looked bewildered. We told her we couldn't cope with it anymore; the fear of losing our baby was overwhelming. We requested that the C-section be done two weeks before the due date. NHS C-sections are usually done only one week before the due date, whereas privately a woman can have one up to three weeks before the due date as long as the baby is big enough.

We had had an ongoing argument with the midwives when calculating the due date, because my periods are every twenty-six days rather than twenty-eight, and the formula used to calculate it needed to be adjusted. Dr Bewley agreed that we were correct and moved my due date to two days earlier. After many months of frustration, meeting a knowledgeable and experienced doctor gave me some sense of peace. Why couldn't everybody be like her?

Dr Bewley told us we were going to get extra doctor's appointments and another ultrasound scan. We left feeling more reassured. It was a countdown now. We had a magic date: 29th of October.

I had a little less than a month to go. I had decided to start my maternity leave early to avoid any more commuting, catching viruses, and generally moving around. I was rather big, so spent those final weeks at home making pancakes for breakfast and lying on the sofa, watching daytime television with a purring Treacle, who, despite my big belly, had no idea of what was coming to her.

Kylie, who I had been seeing routinely during the pregnancy, told me I didn't need to see her anymore. I was going to be fine. I should put my feet up and enjoy it.

We had a further scan to check on the baby and the amniotic liquid. The baby looked all right; doctors concluded that the excessive amniotic liquid was probably caused by the size of the baby rather than something more sinister.

I was relieved to hear the baby was fine. I had the C-section booked. We were ready to go, and at this point, the most funny thing started to happen: every time I shared with somebody that I was having an elective C-section, I was told how lucky I was. That was a surprise. I thought I was meant to be a failure, too weak, too posh to push. Many neighbours, friends, and relatives told me that they had tried and failed to get a C-section. Others had paid for it. I was most surprised by how many men told me that 'it was the right thing to do; the civilised way of doing it'. I wondered, if men could have children, how many of them would opt for drug-free natural birth? It was curious the way people told me, in low tones, as if sharing a secret, something that it was better other people didn't know about you.

What surprised me more than anything else was my grandmother's reaction when I spoke to her. All my life, I had heard tales of her four deliveries at home, on the kitchen table (because, in real life, babies were born on the kitchen table if you didn't want to ruin the mattress with blood and pregnancy fluids) and her repeated tagline: "It was oh so easy! Push for a little time and the baby will pop out."

I called her to let her know, a bit nervous in case she

judged me to be weak. She replied: 'Oh, that's really good! In truth, much better. You're lucky. Giving birth was extremely painful.'

We were called to have a meeting in hospital about the C-section to give us an overview of what was going to happen on the day. My jaw dropped when we arrived and saw the same midwife who had given us the chat about breastfeeding. This time, she gave us the wrong information about my C-section: wrong about stitches, wrong about pre-op tests, post-op details, and wrong about who to contact about a private wing at the hospital. Luckily, we had our leaflets, and we were in any case going to have a final meeting with an obstetrician, who could answer our questions.

After the meeting, we walked to the private wing of the hospital to get the information we needed. Insurance policies do not cover the birth; on the other hand, once a woman has given birth, they will cover the cost of a private room for the time in hospital – a standard three nights unless there are complications. Although medically it made no difference, I valued the fact that I could have privacy and quiet rather than sharing a room with three other women and their babies.

The day before my daughter was born, I could not stop revisiting my previous miscarriages and my babies who did not make it. In the end, I told myself I was going to dedicate that day to them without feeling guilty, since I was not going to have the time to do it when the new baby arrived. I thought they deserved my time.

Birth

C – section

We couldn't wait for the big day to arrive. At our last doctor's appointment, we met Dr Peppas. She seemed warm and cheerful and answered all of our final questions. She told me the cut on my belly would be the standard length of 20cm and that the whole procedure would take about thirty minutes. She asked us what day of the week I was having the C-section.

'Wednesday.'

'Oh! It's going to be me doing your C-section. I do the Wednesday ones.' For no real reason, I had assumed Dr Bewley would be in charge of all the C-sections and she was going to be the doctor at the theatre. I had to change the face I had in mind, and that made me nervous at an already delicate time for me. I said, 'Oh dear.'

'Oh dear why?' said Dr Peppas.

'Oh dear, I am so thrilled it's you and it's finally happening,' I lied. It was a lucky coincidence that we had met Dr Peppas, who made us feel relaxed once the new information sank in, because we could put a name and a face to our doctor.

During the meeting, we also spoke to a lady who was looking for volunteers to donate a piece of uterus cut during their C-section for research on difficult pregnancies. I agreed without giving it a second thought. Michael didn't want me to do it; he looked at me, wondering if I had not been through enough already. If I advocate for more research to be done on miscarriage, I should be the first to volunteer on those few occasions when I can offer some help.

At all the ultrasound scans since week thirty of the pregnancy, we were told that the baby was short (by measuring the length of her femur), and she also had a big round belly. She was a little round meatball. I didn't mind that my daughter was going to be short, below the 40 per cent percentile. Dr Peppas, after reading the measurements, estimated that the baby was too heavy to be a girl; she advised us to be prepared for a boy. We knew she was a girl.

The day before the birth, I was allowed an early dinner, after which I could drink water until midnight. The operation had been scheduled for seven in the morning. When we arrived at the hospital promptly by six a.m., we were told that our designated waiting room, for high-risk pregnancies, was overcrowded; because of this, we would have to wait in a different waiting room, attached to another set of midwives and doctors, in the low-risk pregnancy ward.

As we waited for the operation, Michael kept asking the midwives in our current reception area what was going on. He was repeatedly told that they were aware of us waiting there and were in constant communication with the other team. After several hours without food or drink, when we were more than tired of waiting, he went to the high-risk ward and discovered they had never been told about us. He came back to check with the first lot why this had not happened and had been assured the problem was that they were still busy on the other ward. They had nothing to add except that they were working on a rota.

Chloe, a marvellous midwife

In the end, when the misunderstanding had been sorted out, they were truly sorry (of course) and, after roughly ten hours of waiting, we were moved to a different section within the non-risk pregnancy area, where we had to wait for a theatre to become free. I was weary, hungry, and thirsty; every time I went to the loo, I wet my lips with water. I was considering asking whether I could go home, have some dinner, sleep, and start again the following morning.

Michael went out to get a quick bite to eat. There was no need for both of us to go hungry. While waiting, I started talking to Chloe. She was a new midwife in her first job after university and had been working there for less than a week. She had never delivered a baby or been present at a C-section. Chloe sounded sweet and nice.

All at once, Dr Peppas appeared in a rush. 'Why are you waiting here?' she said. 'You should be in the other ward. You were due at seven a.m., my first C-section of the day.' She told us she had a theatre ready, along with the anaesthetist and all the other theatre staff, but we had to wait for a specialist Thames midwife to join us.

Dr Peppas said, "Now that I have found you, do not to go anywhere else and get misplaced again. Keep waiting here while I sort things out, and we will take to theatre from here." While talking to Chloe about not finding an available Thames midwife, I mentioned it was a bit difficult to communicate with them since they were on a different floor, in the ward where we had all our regular meetings. Chloe said the midwives I had met didn't help with the births; they either did pregnancy appointments or attended the birth, but they didn't do both.

Dr Peppas came back after half an hour and moved us to the high-risk pregnancy section to wait. Still no Thames midwife, so she asked whether I was happy to have Chloe: 'She has no experience, she isn't a Thames midwife, but you've been talking to her this afternoon and seem to be getting on okay.' I said I was pleased to have Chloe. Why not? The midwife was only going to clean the baby. Sure, Chloe was more than capable of doing it. She was kind and sweet. She would do well. We were a complete team at last. Chloe went to get ready.

The most beautiful moment of my life

A nurse appeared after a few minutes to tell us to go to theatre number five; all was ready for us. We made our way there by ourselves. I walked barefoot wearing only a hospital gown; my pregnancy bag was still on the other ward. What a thrill.

I was told off outside the theatre when somebody saw me arrive: 'You shouldn't be barefoot. If you step on something sharp, you'll sue us.' I told her clean hospitals do not have sharp things lying around on corridor floors. We knocked on the door of theatre number five.

I introduced myself: 'Hello, I am the pregnant woman'.

'We can see that,' a voice replied.

The operating theatre was not what I expected. I had assumed it would be a quiet, scary room that smelled strongly of disinfectant. There were many people there, all super friendly. They said hello and introduced themselves. They had music playing on an iPod. It was a joyful place.

Before we started, the anaesthetist told me how much I wanted to be told about the procedure as it was going on.

'Explain it to me just as if I were a five-year-old,' I said.

'Okay,' he replied, 'everything is going to be all right.'

'Good, that's all I need to know.'

He was an extremely pleasant and caring anaesthetist. I didn't notice any of his injections or tubes around my body. The notoriously nasty epidural was painless.

I lay down on the operating table. Michael was on the left-hand side of the table next to me. The anaesthetist and his assistant were on the right-hand side, next to a couple of large monitors. I was asked if I needed Chloe next to me for reassurance. I said I was fine and felt totally calm. There was already a little party of people all around my head.

A small curtain that covered me from my ribs down

was raised to hide my eyes from what was happening on the other side. Dr Peppas' last words before she started were, once again, 'I think it's too big to be a girl. I'll tell you at once if it is a boy.'

'Fine, but she's a girl – Victoria.'

We started. While I was lying there, I felt myself go faint a few times, and instantly, the doctor's voice would say 'shoot' or something similar. The anaesthetist would shoot some more stuff into the drip, and I would perk up instantly. The music was still playing, and a country song came on next. Somebody started complaining about the owner of the iPod's bad taste in music. 'Could we get a better play list on?' several voices said.

I had nothing to do; I did not want to envision the medical details of what was going on. I kept repeating to myself: 'Do not think about it. Do not think about it.'

Unaware of my worries, the anaesthetist told me in a reassuring tone: 'You're doing well. They are almost done getting the amniotic liquid out. Shoot!'

Then I heard Dr Peppas say, 'Put the curtain down.'

Without warning, there she was, my little girl – with enormous eyes staring everywhere and at everybody, moving her head left and right, looking confused. She had inch-long black hair – neither Michael nor I have black hair – and she was covered in muck from head to toe. What a moment: the most beautiful moment of my life, which I will treasure forever. Tears came to my eyes. She was there, she was perfect, she was alive.

Mine in perpetuity. My little daughter. My little strong daughter who had survived my hormonal, malfunctioning body.

It was the most extraordinary moment; at the same time, a shockingly life-changing moment. I'd just had a baby. I had been holding on for months, waiting until I could see her, alive and out of my body. Until that moment, my mind did not want to completely believe it was going to happen. I could finally fully celebrate my child. I understood I was responsible for the wellbeing of this little person for the rest of my life. My previous life was history.

Dr Peppas acknowledged that the baby was, in fact, a girl. Michael was invited to help clean her and cut the umbilical cord. He had been quietly nervous about the C-section – he is more squeamish than me. He had remained sitting next to me the whole time, on the safe side of the curtain. However, he jubilantly got up to go help with Victoria without realising he was about to see my open tummy. He told me, once we were in our room alone, that it was distressing to be confronted with that view of my insides. I didn't want to be told the details; I was willing to do it all again.

Victoria was cleaned and measured by Chloe. Our baby was 54 centimetres tall, which is over the 100 per cent of the usual percentile; she was quite thin – 50 per cent of the percentile. She looked thin and long. The little meatball was more like spaghetti.

It was a magical moment when I could finally hug her in my arms.

Umbilical cord

We had paid two thousand pounds to keep Victoria's umbilical cord. Money well spent – or ideally, money entirely wasted. But if the situation arises that my daughter, or we, or even a close relative gets gravely sick, we could hugely benefit from it; it could literally be a lifesaver. Cord blood stem cells can repair, regenerate, and save lives; for example, they have been used successfully to treat children with leukaemia. Scientists believe that cord blood stem cells will be of great use in the near future in regenerative medicine for many incurable diseases.

The company we used was called Cells4Life. There are a few others on the market. The kit we needed for the process was sent a few weeks before the birth. It got a bit scary when we read the instructions. We had to extract the blood from the umbilical cord with a syringe; it is essential to do it properly, as the more blood you get out the better. The hospital or doctors have no obligation to help. In our case, Dr Peppas did it for us. Many thanks go to her. Michael was ready to do it, but apparently it is not easy to get out all the blood.

Afterwards, we had to call the company right away. A motorbike courier was sent to pick up the kit within the hour. A few days later, we received a call to let us know everything had been stored successfully. At the time, I heard of some hospitals that preferred to keep umbilical cords for their own research. It is something worth discussing with the hospital during pregnancy.

Where to place a woman having a miscarriage?

The whole birth took less than one hour, and afterwards, the three of us – Michael, Victoria, and I – were taken to a post-operation area to rest for three hours as standard procedure. While I couldn't see anybody else there, because all the beds including ours had curtains pulled around them, I could hear a doctor telling two women in the third term of their pregnancies that their babies were dead. The doctor was explaining to them what to do next.

I remembered being in hospital in Spain after my second miscarriage, when I could hear the crying of new-born babies and the happiness and laughter of relatives coming to meet them for first time. As these two women had to listen to this terrible news, they could hear our baby, who had decided it was time to test her lungs.

I was heartbroken for these two invisible women. Should we have been there on the ward together? Maybe there was no other appropriate space in hospital to place us separately. Every time I suffered a miscarriage, I wanted to be miles away from any baby since the pain and memories were too painful to deal with. It had been cruel to be near another baby when I had just lost my own.

Walk of fame

After the three hours in the post-operation area, it was our turn. It was time for our walk of fame. It was the moment to celebrate, to be proud and emotional. To see all those faces turning in awe to look at me and my baby. I had made it. *We* had made it. We were winners. We had our perfect baby. I still get emotional when I recall that moment.

After that, I was taken to my private room. I was pleased I had my own space and that Michael was allowed to sleep there too for the first night. He was given a bed and was able to help with Victoria. It was too late to give us any dinner. We were offered toast, which tasted glorious after a day without food.

A midwife came with us to our room to ask whether I would prefer to be in the other, non-private wing, in a ward with four other women so I didn't feel lonely. I was not feeling lonely at all. I had my little family with me and my own bathroom.

The midwife also wanted to give me morphine for the pain after the C-section. She insisted I'd had invasive surgery and should have morphine, without being ashamed of asking for it to help with the horrible pain. However, I had been given strong painkillers during the operation and I had to assert myself with her, repeating I was in no pain. I was not only in no pain, I was in heaven.

During my three days on the private ward, I came across some excellent midwives. The common strand between them was their age: the older the better, specifically the ones who'd had children themselves. It was only the experienced ones, those who were also mothers, who gave me valuable advice.

Chloe also came to say hello the next day and to see Victoria, which was jolly nice of her.

It was quiet in my corridor, and the only excitement of the three days was when a midwife came the morning after the C-section to remove all the tubes coming out of my belly. She pulled them so hard that I screamed. Next, she removed (badly) the drip on my left hand. Right after she did it, she went to check my blood pressure. I was asked to sit on the bed and not move. She put the blood-pressure arm cuff on the same arm where the drip had been. I sat on the bed, staring at my baby on my right side and at the ceiling to pass the time. When I looked to my left, there was a thin fountain of blood coming out of my left hand, rising about a metre high. It was going everywhere – bed, floor, my clothes. The midwife screamed and three other midwives came running into my room.

There was frantic activity, removing the blood pressure monitor, all my clothes, the bedsheets, trying to clean the floor and not let me see what was going on. I was stripped of my gown, given a new one, and then ushered out of the room. To be fair, I had no idea myself that something like that could happen. It was rather spectacular.

All the midwives I had met on my antenatal appointments had been in their early twenties and inexperienced, just out of university, pretty, wearing plenty of jewellery that jiggled around – I did wonder whether all that jewellery was practical when helping a woman give birth – and most important of all, with no children of their own and no first-hand experience of being pregnant themselves or giving birth. 'I don't know,' was the usual answer to my questions, 'you'll have to talk to a doctor about that.' However, the older, more experience ones I met once I'd had my baby were fantastic.

I had no other physical problems after the C-section; Kylie had been working on that too. I was soon happily walking along the corridors once all the tubes were out, not like a few women who had to be taken around in a wheelchair because, they said, they were torn so badly and had so many stitches they couldn't walk. Some of them looked like they could do with the morphine.

I had bought all sorts of items recommended in magazines to put on after the C-section, which I never used. I was told I was not going to be able to carry the baby around, which I was effortlessly doing. I had some pads to put on top of the scar in case the baby kicked it; I was rather concerned about that, but she never did. She was still doing the same stretching movement she had been keen on before her birth. I carried her with her head on my right shoulder because that was how she liked it. She was too short, anyway, to reach the scar. I had bought some funny granny post-C-section knickers too, which I decided not to use.

I will not tell a woman what to do or judge her on her decision. There is no right or wrong; it is what works for you. I had a C-section because it was what I wanted. Ever since the miracle of life was first explained to me, I haven't thought women get a fair deal. I was only ten years old and already very aware that I was discriminated against in many life situations because I was a girl. I was the *weaker sex* that had to be told what to do. Nearly thirty years later, the advice was still very similar: we women must suffer. In which other situation would a person arrive in hospital and be advised not to have pain killers, to man up?

NICE (National Institute for Health and Care Excellence) guidance says women should be allowed to opt for an elective C-section; however, only a quarter of hospitals complied with the advice. This is despite reports in Spring 2019 that the cost of gynaecological and obstetric cases accounts for nearly half of the claims against the NHS and the cost of negligence was found to be nine times higher for a vaginal birth than a planned C-section.

Postnatal experiences

Breastfeeding pressure

I owe my sanity to the experienced midwife who said it was okay to give Victoria a bottle.

The corridors in our hospital were full of artistic photographs of women with a breast on display, either feeding a baby or with the baby in their arms about to be fed. They all looked glamorous and artistic, like pretty medieval Virgin Marys.

I was very keen on breastfeeding – despite the hospital seminar. We even bought a nursing chair (to this day the most expensive chair in the house). My mother-in-law bought me pretty cover-ups to wear while breastfeeding the baby. I couldn't wait to sit on my comfortable chair and relax with the baby on my breast, as glamorous as those hospital photographs.

In fact, I willingly put Victoria on my breast from the first moment I held her in my arms. But nothing came out. The midwives kept telling me I wasn't doing it properly. They moved the baby up, then down, then closer, then farther away, changed breasts, changed my posture. They kept shaking my breasts roughly and painfully squeezing my nipples.

After trying for over an hour, I would be given a bottle of milk that Victoria would accept ferociously. I kept trying; my mother, Michael, and the midwives all told me how important it was. I lost count of the number of times my nipples were squeezed, the number of times I was told by everybody around me that I was failing; that it was important for my daughter's health that I breastfed her; how it was super easy, I was just not doing it right and had to try harder. I tried a breast pump on several occasions; it didn't produce any milk either.

I had an appointment within the hospital to do a standard check-up on the baby the day after she was born. While I was waiting in a corridor, I could overhear a young girl giving a talk to ten new mothers, declaring she would never,

ever, under no circumstances give one of her future babies any formula milk. Never. A woman asked, 'What if you can't breastfeed? What if the baby needs extra milk?' The answer was the same: never ever.

On my second night in hospital, when I was on my own and Victoria had been crying for hours, an older midwife – and mother of three children – came to my room to ask what was going on. She told me I needed a rest and took the baby away after asking me if she could give her some milk. I said yes. She came back half an hour later. She said Victoria was so hungry she had three times the amount she would normally have. In the end, she had to take the bottle away from Victoria. She assured me there was nothing wrong with feeding the baby that way if the other method was not working. She also told me to put the baby in bed with me. I thought she was insane – everybody else, including other midwives, had said on multiple occasions not to do it. She told me it was fine; I could do it and enjoy it.

Sometimes life sends you a lifesaver – in the middle of the night, alone, when nobody else is up and can hear – when you least expect it.

Before I left hospital to go home, a careless person left an internal folder about me on my bed. I had never seen that folder before. I secretively opened it. I read that they didn't think I was going to be able to breastfeed for a variety of reasons, including the shape of my nipples. I closed the folder and I wished somebody had bothered to talk to me about it. I regret never reading the folder carefully and not confronting somebody about it to clarify the situation.

I asked Michael about my nipples; I had never thought there was anything wrong with them or that they were particularly flat. I should have been looking at women's nipples at the gym changing room rather than minding my business.

During the next two weeks at home I continued trying. I used two different breast pumps for hours and put Victoria on my breasts frequently. Nothing. If I tried with the pump, I could get one drop of watery substance after over one hour, even though it could have been sweat. I was under awful pressure from Michael and my mother: 'keep trying' I was reminded incessantly.

After two weeks of enduring failure, feeling I was the sh*ttiest person ever, and not a drop of milk coming out of my breasts, I said, 'No more trying. Everybody leaves me in peace now!' I was at breaking point. Funnily enough, these are the hardest pages to write in this book.

I am not sure why I was unable to breastfeed, but maybe it was due to my bonkers hormonal body, since I was heavily bleeding for over three months after the birth, or the medication I was on, or my breasts themselves. Maybe I really am useless and nothing works with my body when it comes to pregnancies.

I have since discovered I was not such a unique failure as I assumed I was. A male friend told me he ended up going to the supermarket himself to buy the milk for his wife and baby because she was suffering a nervous breakdown trying to breastfeed when she could not.

I was recently talking to one of my sisters-in-law. She breastfed her two daughters for three months. She had been told word for word the same things. She was in terrible pain with her nipples, which bled constantly. Despite being only breastfed, both daughters had colic – like mine – until they were six weeks old. However, both her daughters had allergy problems while mine does not.

I spoke to a doctor about colic when I couldn't breastfeed the baby. He asserted that colic happens because the intestine is small on a baby; it is only when they grow a bit that colic disappears – the bigger the baby, the quicker it will happen. He told me, 'The person who discovers a cure for colic is going to be a millionaire.'

My sister-in-law said to me that the most annoying thing about becoming a mother was all the fairy tales we were told about breastfeeding, birth, and so forth. We both wished for more respectful, realistic, and bespoke advice.

Two good books I went through when unable to breastfed and feeling down are *Is Breast Best?* by Joan Wolf and *Bottled Up* by Suzanne Barston.

This is not to say I am against breastfeeding, nor do I say that it is not good for you and the baby. However, having read studies about it and going through the scientific data and understanding what the real lifetime risks are, I was able to breathe easier.

Treacle: bitter till doomsday

Three days after Victoria was born, we packed up our baby and suitcase to go back home.

I had spent the last month of my pregnancy lying on the sofa with Treacle, my favourite cute grumpy cat, watching bad morning television. Mainly programs about moving abroad or buying the property of your dreams at a beach resort on a paradisiacal island. Treacle and I came to realise that buying a plot of land in the Caribbean to build a summerhouse was something we needed to consider.

When we parked the car back at home as a family of three, Treacle came to the front door, as she always did, and she saw the baby. She turned the other way straightaway, hurried to the kitchen, and ran out through her cat flap.

Baby born, no more lying on the sofa for me. Treacle was jealous. I tried my best for the three of us to be in one room together. But Treacle was having none of it. She would not be in the same room with Victoria. More dangerously, she would walk around my legs when I was holding the baby in the hallway or going downstairs, making me stumble. Several times I nearly fell over when I got up at night while walking to the nursery room in the dark.

When Victoria grew a bit older, she loved Treacle. Treacle got a bit more accustomed to her but was still jealous. She gave me sad looks; she would leave the room if I hugged or kissed Victoria. In the end, Treacle learnt to live with Victoria and put up with some hugs and patting from her. However, if any other child came into the house, she would run away and we would not see her for hours.

Going to see my boss

My work colleagues could not wait to meet my baby – all but one. There was a naughty reason for it, and I was in it with them. We wanted to see the reaction of our childfree, children-hater boss when I put the baby in her arms. Which I did without asking. It was hilarious. She held Victoria as far away as possible as she could from her body, with straight arms as if she were holding a dangerous weapon that might explode.

I took Victoria back speedily in case she dropped her, and we left with a few departmental winks. I am still laughing about it. That is what I call a successful team-building exercise.

Enormous belly after pregnancy

I wished somebody had told me. The day after Victoria was born, my belly was just as big as before she was born. That meant humongous. Maybe it was not 100 per cent as big as it had been, but it resembled it. After three days in hospital, I came back home and weighed myself – not something any new mother should try at home, for the sake of her blood pressure. When it came to my reaction, think Janet Leigh in *Psycho*. I was only half a kilogram lighter, after having a 3.6 kg baby; plus, having got rid of the placenta, amniotic liquid, and other pregnancy fluids.

It took about a week after the C-section for my body to start getting rid of the pregnancy fluids and related materials. Afterwards, I lost 11kg in two weeks. Every day I was about one kilo lighter. That was the pregnancy weight dealt with, but the weight from the extra pigging out during the pregnancy was there to stay. My belly looked lean during the pregnancy – enormous but nice. Once the baby was out, all the fat congregated around my belly button, like a football sitting in the middle of my stomach. It was distressing.

I had enjoyed my food tremendously during my pregnancy – I can't deny that – but by all appearances I wasn't putting on that much weight. My hips are now that notorious extra inch larger than pre-pregnancy, not from fat, but because their shape has changed. I don't have a strong opinion about this; it just seems to be the way after a pregnancy. So I let it be.

At least after having seen my mother's enormous stretch marks as a little girl, I had been good at using body cream twice a day, every single day of my pregnancy. I did not get a single mark.

Visit from Lambeth employee

After Victoria was born, we had the statutory visit from our local council care worker. I imagine she had more pressing issues to attend to than to come to our house to tell us how to take care of our daughter, considering that we lived in the borough of Lambeth, a deprived area in some parts, which has the largest rate of teenage pregnancy in the whole of Europe.

Never mind all that; here she came to tell us she was going to be Victoria's fairy godmother, looking in on us and checking that we were going to do all the right things, from food to education.

The morning of her visit, we sat in our living-room: husband, baby, the new godmother, and me. She asked me in front of Michael: 'Are you a victim of domestic violence? Does he hit you?' The answer was no, but I reflected: 'Is this how you check a woman's welfare and the baby's safety? By asking a woman in front of her possible abuser if he hits her?' She swiftly ticked the boxes on her paperwork, and then our fairy godmother never showed up again.

Bleeding for three months after birth

After the birth, I was told I might bleed a bit for up to six or eight weeks, which was normal after a pregnancy and nothing to worry about. I was hoping for a follow-up check-up with a gynaecologist at some point.

The bleeding had been more than I was expecting. It was a constant flow and sometimes heavy. I presumed it was going to stop on a few occasions, only for it to become heavy again. I didn't know whether at some point the bleeding could be a regular period starting post-partum. I wondered whether I was having a hormonal problem like in the first miscarriage when I couldn't stop bleeding once I'd got my period. It was definitely heavier than a period; even heavier than in some of my previous miscarriages. I had no previous experience, but my instinct told me it was not normal. However, I had no time to deal with it or ask other women about it. I simply hoped for it to stop.

Only after I had been bleeding for more than eight weeks did I go to the GP. The GP simply said bleeding after pregnancy was normal. However, he never investigated it, asked me any probing questions, or performed any tests.

I also had horrible shoulder pain. Nothing to do with the pregnancy itself. I have a dodgy shoulder – too much time working at a computer and bad posture when sitting in front of it. By then I had not exercised for months, and I very much wanted to be referred to see a physio, because sometimes the pain was so intense that I screamed in bed when rolling over and I couldn't hold Victoria with my left arm. My GP maintained there was no need for me to see a physio; I just needed to exercise my shoulder at home. I was not reassured and came back home to continued bleeding and shoulder pain.

After two more weeks of heavy bleeding, a piece of solid meat came out of my body when I woke up one night to go to the loo. It was a bit more than an inch long. I did not know whether it could be a piece of the placenta or something else that should have come out earlier. Scarier, it could be an early stage foetus of a new pregnancy – since a couple of times we had not been careful.

I put the 'meat' in a container in the freezer. I wanted to be sure it was analysed. I booked myself a private appointment at the London Bridge Clinic with a gynaecologist for a woman's health check. My mother and sisters-in-law told me all women get one in Spain after six weeks of giving birth.

I paid over £400 to find out that the appointment did not include an ultrasound scan – for that I would have to pay an extra £100. What a rip off! This was extraordinarily hard to swallow since the procedure cost €50 to €100 in Spain. I did not take the container with me because I wanted to be sure they could analyse it before I risked it getting damaged. Instead, I took some photographs to show the doctor. The doctor said she could not say for sure what it was without having it there with her. It could have been an early miscarriage or maybe something to do with my previous pregnancy, but she remained noncommittal.

She recommended that I use my health insurance because it would cover the cost of a visit to a gynaecologist now that I was no longer pregnant. I made another appointment at London Bridge Hospital and this time I took the container with me. The gynaecologist claimed it was better for me not to know what it was and threw it away without giving me time to object. She wanted me to do a blood test to check my iron levels and see me again for a second appointment. I didn't see the point of any of that, so I didn't see her again.

I could guess what the piece of meat was if 'it was better for me not to know' an early foetus. I cannot think of anything else that was better for me not to know according now to two gyneacologists. Although maybe the doctors were not completely sure what it was. I am kidding myself they did not know, anything else rather than a firm conviction it was an early foetus would have meant the doctors doing tests both on the piece of meat and myself to rule out any illnesses or health complications . I always believe it is better to know. Knowledge is power. The bleeding stopped completely not long after the piece of meat came out.

My shoulder has remained dodgy for life, though. I can no longer use a computer mouse with my left hand – and I am a leftie. I needed a few rounds of rehabilitation. Eventually, I managed to see a good physiotherapist privately who worked wonders.

Getting engaged

After Victoria was born at the end of October, I wondered whether Michael was going to propose. I was laidback about marriage. It is not a guarantee for a successful relationship. Still, it was at the back of my mind. We had not spoken about it, even casually.

Early in December, after the annual bonus-time weeks

of tension, Michael asked me what I wanted for my birthday and Christmas. I concluded marriage was not on the table since he was asking about presents rather than buying a ring. Lack of ideas on my side was not a problem, in any case. I asked for two items: a Montblanc fountain pen and a sewing machine.

On the morning of my birthday, I opened my birthday card and present while in bed with Victoria. It was the beautiful fountain pen I wanted. Michael said he was hoping for a quiet moment during the day. I thought he was mad, hoping for a quiet moment.

Later, we went out for lunch with Victoria. We went to the same pub where we had decided we wanted to have children. Michael was restless; he went to the loo twice although he hardly ever uses the facilities if we are eating out. I wondered whether he was unwell; it is not that relaxing, going out for lunch with a two-month-old baby.

We came back home. Michael again hoped for a quiet moment at some point in the afternoon. I concluded he was getting disillusioned about quiet moments in a house with a baby and Treacle. While we were out, Treacle left me a birthday present on the bed in the form of a huge pee – to make us aware of her true feelings about the new resident.

At last, Victoria decided she was happy sitting in her baby bouncer in the living-room, after Michael put on Celine Dion singing in French (by mistake). Victoria decided straight away that the sound was very soothing and went to sleep.

Wonderful, we thought, we had found a sleeping method; furthermore, we would be able to embarrass her when she was older about her musical taste. I changed into comfy clothes and slippers. For once, I sat on the sofa to read the newspaper. It was my birthday after all, a special treat. Michael came back after another trip to the loo upstairs. He was definitely unwell, I feared.

Michael sat down next to me. He announced he had one more present for me. I got goose bumps. One more present: *Could it be …?* He told me the present came with a question. *A question? That sounds promising*. I told to myself to wait to hear the question. There are all sorts of possible silly questions that could be asked.

He took out a small parcel hidden in the pouffe. I opened it. There it was, my engagement ring. I asked: 'What is the question?'

'Do you want to marry me?'

'Yes.'

We kissed, we hugged, we were relieved Victoria was peacefully sleeping. We were engaged and thrilled about it. Michael suggested we have another baby first, and afterwards, we could concentrate on organising the wedding.

I told him that was not a good idea. 'I might be too fat for the wedding photos after two children.' He gave me one of those 'you are not selling yourself too well' looks. 'Let's get married soon,' I continued, 'and have another child later on.' All said and done, within seven months we were married. We married in my home town. It was a beautiful sunny day, in a northern Spain town famous for its rain, so it could have gone either way. It was a small wedding with about sixty family members and close friends. My two-year old niece was my flower girl. The wedding preparation was so smooth. I had too many worries in my head about leaving Victoria behind for the honeymoon, when I was going to find another job, childcare, to get stressed about a wedding, even my own wedding! I'd bought a dress that I'd seen on a window display while on a walk. I flew with Victoria to Spain ten days before the wedding and chose the flowers, bouquet, car, and everything else on the spot. We had a very friendly priest who looked very confused when everybody laughed when he said, 'maybe God will bless them one day with a child'. He whispered to me what was going on and when I told him, he lifted his arms and said loudly, 'God has already blessed them with a baby!'

Getting an au pair

When Victoria was seven months old, we realised it was time to start organising some help at home for when I had to go back to work and so we would have some free time for ourselves and be able to go out occasionally. I was very reluctant to do it. The idea of somebody taking care of my baby was frightful. Victoria had such a strong character; I didn't want anybody shaking her in anger.

We decided to look for a Spanish au pair, who could help Victoria grow up bilingual. Somehow, we didn't manage to find anybody from Spain, although there were meant to be hundreds of girls wanting to come over to England. We found an agency that looked well organised, although they provided only Swedish au pairs. After reading about the positives and negatives of having a young girl in the house, it was crystal clear that the *crème de la crème* were the Swedish girls, who are generally responsible, mature, calm, and treated children with a lot of respect, plus they speak good English.

Families are not allowed to leave an au pair for more than two hours alone with a baby younger than two years old, we learnt. If I was going back to work, we needed an 'au pair plus'. This was somebody older, with previous experience with babies, who had to be paid a higher weekly amount because of the extra responsibility.

We interviewed five girls and settled upon Evelina, who agreed to come to us if her Swedish boyfriend could come over and stay in the house to visit her. We were surprised by the request. She was in her early twenties and she had the right to have a boyfriend, so we agreed, even if we were not completely sure about it. In the end, the boyfriend, a very nice man, came to visit once or twice. However, their relationship did not survive the distance.

When we picked her up from the airport, I saw she was a great choice. We wanted to give her a few days to get used to the house and us. However, on her second day, she said she wanted us both to go out for dinner. She had no concerns about staying by herself with Victoria, making her food, bathing her, and putting her to bed. We went out to a nearby restaurant, where we put both our phones on the table – on the few occasions we had tried to leave Victoria with my mother, things did not go smoothly because Victoria often got unsettled and my mother kept changing Victoria's routine, who from a very early age knew what and when she wanted something. When we came back home all was quiet; the evening had been easy. Victoria was happy with her.

MISCARRIAGE NUMBER THREE
The Confident Couple

During the final stages of my pregnancy, I considered it wise to have a proper investigation into the APS issue and my general wellbeing. I didn't want the worry at the back of my mind about whether I was ill. Was I going to get ill in the future due to this clotting issue?

I asked a midwife at the maternity department at St Thomas' whether they could give me a referral, as I wasn't sure which department to contact within the hospital. I was given an appointment with the haematology department and had another blood test not long after Victoria was born. A couple of months later, I received a letter with an appointment date. I wanted to make it into a day out for Victoria and me; I hadn't yet used public transport with her and the buggy. I couldn't walk to our usual station because it had no lift or escalator and the station had two long flights of deep steps. We went to the next station further down the line.

As we got into the train, tiny Victoria was awake. I reckoned it would be a good idea to get her out of her buggy and sit her on my lap. That way, she could look through the window and it would be easier to keep her entertained. The train was fast, as they usually are, and Victoria's eyes went swirling, whirling fast. She got upset and started to cry loudly.

That was my first – mortifying – mother-and-child commuting experience. I had every commuter on the train staring at me with hate. I wish they would dare to look like that at antisocial teenagers. It was difficult to sit down and keep calm. People's looks made me ashamed of myself: *I know nothing; such a terrible mother; what a silly thing to do to take her out of the buggy to look through the window.* I stood up with Victoria and moved as far as I could from everybody else in the carriage. I considered getting off the train to wait for the next one, but I didn't want to be late for the appointment. I stayed put.

When we at last arrived at Victoria Station, I let everybody get off before us. My fellow passengers left giving me looks of loathing. I was grateful that, at least, nobody said anything nasty to me.

From the station, I walked to St Thomas'. I could have extended my travel experience by getting the bus, but I'd had enough of public transport for the day. When we arrived in hospital, we went up to the haematology department, where I was told by the receptionist to sit down and wait for my name to be called. I was not asked who I was. After waiting for an hour, I went back to the receptionist. I told her I was still there waiting. I handed in the letter I had in my handbag. She checked on her computer.

She said, 'Didn't you receive a new letter from us? Your appointment has been moved to next week.'

'No, I did not receive any new letter from you. Is there

anything you can do since I'm here already?'

'No, you will need to come back next week.'

I grabbed baby and buggy and walked – furiously – back to the station. This time, when on the train, I kept Victoria away from windows and trouble.

A week later, I turned up for my appointment, minus my baby on this occasion, who was at home with our cleaner, who was happy to babysit. My appointment was with a young female doctor. She was wearing loads of rattling bracelets that jingled during our conversation every time she moved her arms. Her words and the bracelets noise mixed together in my head. She told me I had a bad illness; the same variable that had tested positive with Mr Mackay was positive again by just one number above the normal values.

She told me that flying was high-risk for me. I should never go on a plane without having an injection first and needed daily medication for the rest of my life. She told me that my illness, ultimately, would kill me. I could have a blood clot at any time. I could be living on borrowed time already. A numb sensation came over me. It was a death sentence.

I foresaw my poor motherless baby and Michael being left all by himself with our child. I could not understand how I could be mortally ill; I had never noticed anything during all the long-haul flights I had sat through without moving for hours. I had to fight back the tears.

When the doctor wanted me to book a follow-up appointment, I told her I would do it at the reception desk on my way out, although I had no intention of doing so. Instead, I ran for it. I left hospital with a severe pain in my chest, imagining the rest of my – short – life.

By the time I arrived home, I started to disagree with everything I had been told by her. I'd had two blood tests, both done soon after a miscarriage and a pregnancy, with the possible lower indication of a tendency for blood clotting in one of three possible variables, There are 3 variables that need to be above a value to confirm the condition, in my case it was only one out of three. If a normal value of up fifteen on the scale the doctor was using, my result was seventeen, on an scale up to over forty. Any pregnancy, successful or unsuccessful increasing these results and the change of false positives, that's why the tests should not be done right after a pregnancy. In both positive cases, I had been severely stressed out for completely different reasons; that is what I could not control: my overheating mind. Then I'd had two or three further blood tests, indicating that I didn't have any signs of APS. This variable, I read, can give a false positive after very stressful events or pregnancies, as a result of the changes during the pregnancy, which was when I'd had these two particular blood tests.

Weeks later, I was referred by the hospital to the lupus department at St Thomas'. They deal with expectant women with antiphospholipid syndrome – and many other related conditions to APS. For my first meeting, I was lucky to meet the Head of the Department. She told me I was not dying, I did not have any long-term illness, and – more importantly – I did not have APS. There was no need for me to have any regular medication and there was no more risk for me than for any other person of getting a blood clot. Nevertheless, I had problems with pregnancies, and the APS treatment had worked before for me with Victoria. Therefore, the right thing to do was to repeat that treatment for future pregnancies. My so-called lucky pants treatment. We had a great conversation. She told me how surprised she was about my extensive knowledge of APS. By then, I had read several books and articles about the subject, guided by Francisco, an old friend from my school years, who is now a renowned immunologist in the USA (I always believed he was going to make it big).

Jumping ahead, after several meetings over three years, after having Victoria and three more miscarriages, with no more tests indicating any sign of APS and after three unsuccessful pregnancies following their advice and medication, it was concluded, by all the doctors, that I did not have APS.

End of the maternity year

After having Victoria, there was no question as to whether we were going to have another child. *One* is such a solitary number. I even like to place at least two plants together in a room. That way they can keep each other company. There was not much discussion either about when; better sooner rather than later. The children would be of a similar age, and they could play together.

We had agreed to get married and have a second baby soon afterwards. Michael wondered whether, if I got pregnant during my maternity leave, I could carry on with a second maternity leave without going back to work. I was not convinced I would be entitled to link two maternity leaves together. I could imagine people's faces if I came back to work with another big bun in the oven.

That said, I remembered my friend Silje from Norway, who was six months pregnant when she went for a job interview. She got the job, worked for two months, and then had fully paid maternity leave for about two years – as is standard in that country. (She is also allowed two hours during the working week in which to go to the gym or exercise to keep healthy, and working overtime is forbidden.) The Norwegian government has changed the maternity leave package. It was made compulsory that at least three months of paternity leave should be taken by the dad. Otherwise, they would lose the time off as a family. Brilliant. If any man going for an interview could conceivably take a number of paternity leaves during his career, maybe this would slightly reduce the discrimination against women. Or maybe it would go the other way in England, and husbands would have to stop wearing their wedding rings to job interviews.

I had a job interview in July, one week before travelling to Spain for our wedding. Telling the interview panel that I was on maternity leave was not a clever move. I was not going to mention Victoria, and I took off my engagement ring. The first question I was asked was: 'What have you been doing at work for the last year? What are your mayor achievements in the previous twelve months?', which took me by surprise. I should have thought about it – and been prepared to lie about my activities. They could have already known I'd had a baby if they had contacted my boss, as many companies like to do before interviewing a candidate.

However, I do not like lying. 'For the last year I have been on maternity leave,' I said. 'However, I can tell you what I did *before* my maternity leave.' I had an amazing number of work achievements to share with them. All the same, I saw their faces and the discreet looks at one another. I was out. I felt so stupid. It was such a good job, closer to our house.

I spent over nine months looking at job sites daily. I could not find any part-time job that looked interesting or had a decent salary that allowed to pay for childcare. I was not ready to give up my career. I concluded it was best to get pregnant straight away after going back to work. Once I had my second baby, I would be able to think more clearly, and with no worries about future pregnancies or more babies on the way, I would be able to convince a new company that I was worth investing in. What's more, I would not be taking any maternity leave with them.

Michael told me I didn't need to go back to work. However, I wanted to earn my own money. People might judge that it is not fair on the company, but is it fair on women to be treated as we are?

Days before the wedding, I received an email from my boss, asking me to confirm in writing whether I was coming back to work after my maternity leave. I had always told her I was going to, but maybe she had heard I was looking for another job or perhaps she was hoping for me not to return. Before I'd left on maternity leave, when we were both interviewing for a new web assistant, an interviewee asked about opportunities for promotion and my boss blurted out: 'There is the web manager job.' Which was still mine – as far as I knew.

The next day, I logged back onto my email with a heavy heart to reply to her message. I saw the top email in my inbox – subject: 'we have news for you' from the National Lottery. If only. I crossed my fingers: one million would do. I had won £10. Time to reply to my boss.

I went back to work in September, when Victoria was eleven months old. My work pattern was from seven in the morning to three in the afternoon. It was an hour's commute to work, plus another hour to come back home if the trains were running on time.

I was, to tell the truth, excited to be out of the house and grateful I was allowed to start as early as seven. Victoria used to wake up around nine in the morning, as during her first two years when she was not going to nursery and there was no need to hurry up in the mornings getting up early, I followed a Spanish timetable with her, so she was not in bed until eight or nine at night and could see Michael after work. I was determined to use each minute of the day wisely. I was going to achieve a lot if I had done two hours' work before Victoria woke up. It would mean two hours less in which we weren't together later in the day.

It was good to talk to adults, to put my mind onto something that was not baby related. I acquired some new friends at work, colleagues with children. I found it quite funny to hear an officer over six foot tall, with a crooked nose after years of police work and rugby playing, talking to his little daughter on the phone about her wearing her nice pink knickers and being nice to her baby sister.

I was entitled to use up my annual holiday until the end of the year. I had not been aware of this until I came back to work. It was such a bonus. My boss also let me work one day from home until Christmas, after telling me that she had sacked her own cleaner, because the lady had asked for a week of unpaid leave as her children were on holiday and she had nobody to leave them with. My boss didn't like women with children: 'They think they can do what they like,' she told me. 'At work, it's different,' she said. She had to follow the company rules – not without regret. She routinely worked one day a week from home and claimed she got more done there.

Computer password

The novelty of being back at work faded in no time: I disliked being there, with the same old issues and office politics – I never saw that many depressed adults in any of my other jobs. Nevertheless, I smiled a lot and I tried to convince my new young assistant that our company was an excellent place to work. Lucky us: we were getting invaluable experience at such a reputable place. Sadly, misfortune struck. He needed my computer password for some updates, and I had to give it to him: *'ihatethisplace'*. 'Yes, me too!' he replied.

Victoria was not taking the new arrangements well. Although she was keen on Evelina, she was always stressed out by the time I came home in the early evening. She was clingy and got angry if I had to stop playing with her to make her dinner or do any other chores. She could have an hour-long tantrum almost every day after me being away. Loud, relentless crying and screaming; once she started, she found it difficult to stop. I wanted to give her every minute of my life. I loved her so much, and I didn't spend enough time with her. Work, baby, and trying to get pregnant while keeping an eye on job adverts, just in case the perfect job appeared. It was upsetting and exhausting.

Early one morning when walking to the station, I fainted and fell over, scratching both my knees and one hand. When I told Kylie during my next acupuncture session that I couldn't have any needles on my legs because of my bruises, she replied candidly, 'I hope at least somebody helped you.' Nobody had helped me, but that was because it had happened in a quiet area at about six in the morning, which had spared me the embarrassment of somebody seeing me.

'Why were you in the street that early?' Kylie asked.

'I start work very early before my daughter is even awake, so I can come back home earlier in the day and spend more time with Victoria,' I explained.

Planning ahead

Michael and I were confident about trying for a baby again. This time, we were fully aware of the potential problems, and we had a successful treatment to repeat: injections, the progesterone, and the aspirin. And acupuncture sessions. My bicornuate uterus had managed to carry a large baby until the end of the pregnancy successfully. It could surely do it one more time. The baby would most probably be breech like Victoria, which didn't cause any complications for her. There is a risk that breech babies can be born with problems in their hips. All breech babies have a hip scan six weeks after they are born. Victoria had one too, although it was clear to us and the doctors that her hips where fine.

By this time, Michael's mum had been in and out of hospital for months, each time with a different diagnosis and a set of medications that didn't seem to work. She was deteriorating rapidly. It had started with what looked like breathing problems and had escalated to muscle cramps and difficulty in walking.

My wish to have acupuncture frequently to prepare my body for the new pregnancy was not going well. Between work and running back home, I didn't have time for appointments and only saw Kylie a couple of times before getting pregnant. I was more confident about my body anyway. I was self-assured. I was stronger. I had done it all before; therefore, I was not concerned about the lack of sessions. I was doing my best with the time I was given.

We tried to get pregnant in September, as soon as I was back at work. We failed, which was unexpected. October was a luckier month. I didn't have to wait for the test result: I just knew; experience counts for something. I was pregnant and blessed again, counting the days until the due date. I was sure I would not come back to my current workplace after the pregnancy, for many reasons; firstly because *ihatethisplace* was not a mere password. They didn't like me either – now married and a mother. My boss, who I had been told had been going for interviews for months, would be resentful after I'd taken two maternity leaves. By the end of my second pregnancy, I would have been a manager for six to seven years, a more than justifiable time to move up somewhere else.

Before it had been confirmed that I was pregnant back in October, I got a nasty flu. I was told by the GP it was not going to affect my pregnancy. If I was pregnant, I was safe to have antibiotics, and I recovered nicely. I was poorly for a week, but I got to be at home, which was a bonus. Other than that, we had a private scan to confirm the pregnancy, and we listened to the heartbeat a few weeks afterwards. All was encouragingly positive. It was a waiting game.

The due date for the baby was 12 August. Every morning when I arrived at work, I wrote on the palm of my right hand '12 Aug' to remind me that everything was going to be fine in the end – even if right then the sensation was overwhelming, with everything that was going on at the same time. It was my deadline for happiness: after 12 August, the sun was going to shine beautifully and infinitely. I was going to spend quality time with my babies. I could calm down and resume my career afterwards.

The price of my child's safety

I was excitedly making plans for the future. I had a notebook on my desk, in which I wrote down my life plan and ultimate career path. I was contemplating different options. I had lots of ideas, but some of them needed proper investment. During my maternity leave, I would only be paid most of my salary for the first twelve weeks. After that, it would be around £125 a week until the final three months, when I received no money at all. If I quit altogether and didn't come back, it was uncertain how many months it would take me to find new employment. It was all about money: every day I recalculated how much I could afford to spend and save and how I was going to spend my money wisely.

I was also considering whether to study an MBA in Technology Management with the Open University while at home. It would have been the next step up the ladder for me. I could, one day, work as a freelancer or start my own company, which would have freed me from bosses and allowed me to choose my own hours of work, my comings and goings. I resembled an accountant rather than a web manager at work, spending all day speculating about my finances, adding up sums.

However, I had enough on my plate with Victoria, and I had not even been able to open a book since her birth. I am not sure what made me think that with two children I would have time to study for an MBA, even if it was done online. I read inspirational stories about mothers starting their own companies while having little babies at home by staying up into the early hours and – oh! – how difficult but rewarding it had been in the end for them.

My work telephone rang one morning in November while I was on my own in my office, concentrating on my finances rather than my legitimate work. My pregnancy was still a well-kept secret. It was Evelina. She sounded nervous and kept repeating that she was so, so sorry. Victoria had fallen backwards from the sofa and hit the back of her head on the corner of the living-room glass table. Evelina repeated that Victoria was fine, that there some blood but not much, and that she was crying her eyes out. She could not calm her down. She suggested that maybe I should come home to take Victoria to the GP.

My heart was pumping frantically. I could see my accounts next to me while talking on the phone. *What was the price of my baby's safety and health? How much money exactly did I need in my savings account?* What I needed above all was for my daughter to be safe whatever the cost. I took the train home. It was the longest journey ever. When I arrived, I took Victoria to the GP. She was fine – a nasty bump, and a bit too late for a stitch by the time we made it to the surgery, according to the doctor. *How much money did I need?*

The breakdown

One night in early December, Victoria woke up crying. I had been sleeping on my front and hurried to get up from bed. A sharp stabbing pain on the lower left-hand side of my belly pierced all the way from my front to my back. It felt like I was being stabbed with a long, sharp knife. I asked Michael to get up instead. I couldn't move for two to three minutes. I had to hold my breath. It was the same intensity as the pain in my second miscarriage, although this pain was sharper, while on the other occasion it resembled being pressed by a wide fist. The pain soon went altogether, and I slept calmly for the rest of the night.

A few days later, Kylie, my divine Kylie, told me she

was going to India to do charity work after Christmas. She was going to help women who had been sold as slaves and prostituted for years until they had been rescued. 'Fantastic work!' I congratulated her, but the reality was her news made me sad – selfishly. I was going to be left on my own when I badly wanted her help during my pregnancy months. I needed her on my journey.

By now, it was almost Christmas and my birthday again. The day before I turned thirty-eight years old, a bit of nasty brown discharge appeared. Only once. On my birthday, a Sunday, we took a train trip around London on the famous *Orient Express*, enjoying an early Christmas menu lunch. It was an expensive treat, and I tried to look cheerful and relaxed.

Yet I was feeling uneasy. I kept going to the loo and seeing more spots of brown discharge each time. There was no blood or pain, only the same murky substance that had appeared during my second miscarriage after the nasty bleeding on that occasion. I was in denial: it simply could not be happening again. I was having all the treatments, injections, progesterone, and aspirin as instructed. I had a daughter. I could do it again.

The following Tuesday morning, I got up to go to work. I dragged my feet to the loo. My body opened like a tap turned on full – not of water but of blood. I realised it was over.

We rushed to the Early Pregnancy Unit at St Thomas'. They seemed to be the best bet; they were always responsive. At least our previous bad experiences came in useful; there was no point in calling 111, seeing the GP, going to A&E, or calling the dedicated team of midwives that never called back. The Early Pregnancy Unit was the place to go.

First, we met a young doctor who told us straight away that this was happening because of my age. We asked him about having an investigation into whether I was having a third miscarriage. However, the doctor stated I did not qualify for one because my miscarriages were not consecutive. I was still officially 'unlucky'. He told us we could wait there for an ultrasound scan to see whether there was a heartbeat. I was not considering going to Spain this time if it was confirmed my pregnancy was over. Having a toddler to take care of made travelling more complicated.

Michael had to go to work because it was unclear how many hours I would have to wait. I was fine being on my own; I guess I prefer to be solo in the darkest times – at least I don't need to think of polite conversation. There was nothing anyone could do. I waited for a few hours and kept repeating to myself that a miscarriage had also started with Victoria, and it had stopped. There was a thin line of hope there: maybe there was going to be a heartbeat – although this time the amount of bleeding was heavier and there had been the sharp pain a few days earlier.

I did find out while I was there – by eavesdropping on the conversations of other women who had recently given birth and their doctors – that I should have gone back to the Early Pregnancy Unit to check on the heavy bleeding I'd suffered with for months after giving birth. I could have never guessed, since the name of the department and my situation after the birth did not seem to be a match. It was never too late to learn for a future journey.

There was another woman sitting nearby who had a toddler with her. It was too hot and really busy in the waiting room. The boy was bored and started to have a massive tantrum, throwing himself on the floor. Nobody was angry with him. I think we all wished we had a little tantrum toddler on the way rather than the uncertainty of our situation.

The scan confirmed my fears. The foetus had no heartbeat, the pregnancy was over. Surprisingly, I was told straight away that I could have an ERPC if I wanted one – at least this was not St George's.

It was a long day in hospital. I arrived back home hours after the time I usually did if I had been at work. I hadn't told Evelina I was pregnant or where I had been, just that I was not feeling well and had had quite a busy day. Evelina was crying; she had heard on the news that the airports might close as there was a bit of snow on the way, which Swedish people find difficult to understand, and she was upset as she wanted to go home for Christmas to see her boyfriend. Victoria had got a bit difficult during the day and, being upset herself, Evelina could not calm her. Evelina had called her mum, who got anxious about Evelina walking up and down the hallway with a heavy baby because it was bad for her back. Au pair and baby were both vocal about their misadventures; I had to keep calm and quiet about my own situation.

Emergency list

After the miscarriage was confirmed, I had a conversation with a nurse about the ERPC. I was going to be placed on an emergency list. That way, as soon as there was a bed available, I could have my operation. That sounded good to me. I had to phone the department early every morning to ask whether there were any empty beds that day. Christmas was around the corner; on the one hand, I needed this to be done speedily to *enjoy* Christmas; on the other, I was not hopeful, timewise, that it was going to happen.

I phoned every morning for a few days – no bed available. On Boxing Day, I decided not to phone. I wanted to spend the bank holiday with my family instead. However, I got a call from the hospital to tell me there was a bed available; I had to go there straightaway, which I did. When I arrived, the four beds in my room were empty. I was told to wait for a doctor to come. I changed into a hospital gown, nervously waiting for news.

I had been there by myself for about four hours, when finally a cheerful doctor appeared, She said, 'Why are you here on Boxing Day? We're not going to be able to do anything today.' I was not amused. She asked me to wait while she double-checked in case they could fit me in somewhere.

She came back after two hours to confirm, 'No, it's

not going to be possible.' She suggested that I could keep waiting if I wanted to, but realistically it was not going to happen. She pointed out that I shouldn't be on an emergency list anyway, because people coming to hospital with more serious conditions would always have priority, which was fair enough. Anybody in a traffic accident, having a heart attack, and so forth was always going to be in front of me because the number of operating theatres was limited and doctors need to prioritise the most urgent cases. I should have been on a list for *day surgery*, which would give me an exact date and time for the operation.

She left to ask for a day surgery appointment, and I was given 30 December. That was good news; it meant I could leave it all behind me before the New Year and have a fresh start. I changed into my clothes, packed my things, and went back home.

The bad ERPC/SMM

When the day arrived, I needed to be in hospital early in the morning, having had no food or drink since dinner the previous day. All the patients having surgery on that day needed to arrive at the same early time. No visitors or chaperons were allowed. We were all given a hospital gown to put on. Everything was taken away from us: no mobile, no food, no magazines to read, no going out and coming back later. Unsure of the reason for this, I reckoned it was a bit extreme, but those were the rules. I imagined things were going to move fast and it was important for patients to be ready.

I was informed that my operation was scheduled to be the last one of the day; I was left there for several hours – incommunicado – concerned that Michael would be trying to call me. In the end, after over five hours in an increasingly empty room, it was my turn to go in.

This time, I had not been given any pills to insert. That was a huge relief. I had no physical objections with waiting there for that many hours. Again, if other people were in pain or had more complicated issues, they should go first. It was the mental issues: waiting in a room for more than half a day, isolated, without nothing to do but mourn my dead baby while thinking of the operation ahead. I missed not to have something to read but was told I could not access my belongings until I was ready to leave.

The anaesthetist was sympathetic, and before putting me to sleep, he told me his daughter had suffered a miscarriage too. He understood it was a devastating experience. I woke up to emptiness, a bare physical body, and broken illusions. I did not get to see the surgeon who was going to perform the operation. It was quick, the standard twenty minutes.

I woke up shortly afterwards, and the hospital phoned Michael to let him know I was ready to be picked up. Patients are not allowed to leave by themselves – not even in a taxi. I could go after the customary sandwich and wee. I could not be released until I could eat and go to the loo without getting sick. Eventually, I was authorised to leave with a large number of painkillers, along with a doctor's note giving me a week off work. I was entitled to further time off by visiting the GP if I needed longer to recover, which I was advised was common.

I was not up for sharing the latest miscarriage at work, as I had not told them I was pregnant in the first place. I ignored the sick note and went back to work three days later, on 2 January, at the end of my holiday period. I wanted to keep everything private and move on. This proved not to be wise, though. I was not well and was in a lot of pain; daily intense period pain. I was exhausted. I needed a rest for all sorts of reasons. In the end, I needed painkillers for three months. In fact, the pain only stopped when I got pregnant once more.

Dr Russell's blood pressure

St Thomas' confirmed that they would not do any tests on me, regarding my three non-consecutive miscarriages, so I was still officially only an 'unlucky' person. However, they would analyse the foetus to see if that could give us any clues. Commonly, a miscarriage occurs when there is something wrong with the foetus, Doctors reminded me, 'our bodies are clever. They would not go ahead with a pregnancy that is not viable if there were any genetic issues'.

We received a letter for an appointment at Guy's Hospital over two months after the ERPC to tell us the results. I wasn't sure why the appointment was at Guy's. However, since both hospitals are part of the same trust, we assumed the specialists or labs were over in that building.

We had a proper *Carry On* comedy doctor's appointment.

We arrived, Michael and I, at the Obstetrics Department at Guy's one afternoon to find a long-suffering Dr Russell. He was stressed out because of the large number of patients waiting to be seen and apologetic to us for the nearly two-hour waiting time. Dr Russell had my file but there was no information regarding the test results – even though the tests are routinely done within twenty-four hours of an ERPC since the pregnancy remains start to decompose in a short space of time. Somehow, the results had not been added to my file or to the hospital computer system either. There was a medical student with the doctor in his office; we agreed he could stay to listen.

I can only be grateful to Dr Russell, who was frantically phoning everybody who, he reasoned, could help. He kept reading through my file, looking for any useful information to give us. When, eventually, he managed to get hold of somebody in the lab, he was told that, on the grounds of patient confidentiality, we could not get the results over the phone. Dr Russell explained that we were in the hospital with him and they could talk to us since he was calling internally, as they could see by the numbers on their phone. Also, if they preferred, they could call us back. They we having none of it.

At long last, the lab agreed to fax the results. Only for the faxes on our side not to work. After over an hour of him arguing with everybody and screaming every time he was put on hold, 'My blood pressure! The NHS is ruining my blood pressure!' he was told briefly, 'All was well with the foetus.' Apart from being dead, of course. As far as we knew, it was a healthy baby.

While the doctor was out of the room, checking the fax, the medical student told us he preferred ophthalmology.

THE IMAGINARY BUN

Over the years, I have spent a ridiculous amount of money on pregnancy tests, trying to confirm a pregnancy when it was far too early to test. There was a bright bedside lamp in our room; I would take the test and place the stick over it to see whether I could identify an evasive, translucent cross days before it was due to appear. 'Try the pregnancy test first thing in the morning', the leaflet recommends. I couldn't wait until morning. I would invariably use the test in the evening as soon as I arrived home. Later in the evening, I would drive back to the supermarket to purchase a new one to use in the morning.

It takes weeks for the body to get rid of all the pregnancy hormones. I have learnt that from hard experience. Even after a miscarriage, the body needs time to return to its normal regular levels; not necessarily the same number of weeks each time, as experience has also taught me.

Back at work after our eventful Christmas, and in pain, I appreciated there was a good reason for having a week off after the operation. However, it seemed more important to keep silent about it and not get signed off.

Michael and I were troubled and depressed. We did not understand where the problem lay. We had been certain this pregnancy was going to be all right, after having Victoria and because we were using the same treatment. It was all taking its toll on us. There was no time for us as a couple to relax between work, Victoria, pregnancies, and stress. I was running out of annual leave and ideas for how to plan our future. I was back at work full-time; four days at the office and one at home. Evelina started complaining about her long week. She found the job boring, as well as isolated, 'because babies are cute, but they don't talk much'.

We received some devastating news during the days that followed. Michael's mum, Erika, who had not been well since Victoria's birth, was confirmed to be suffering from motor neurone disease (MND) and given approximately two years to live. She was willing to stay in her house. However, with every week that passed by it became clearer that it was not going to work for her and she would have to move to a specialist care home. She was such an active, independent woman, in her seventies, studying for a university degree, writing a book, riding her bicycle every day, and she had even parachuted from a plane not that long before.

Michael's dad – long-time divorced from his mum – started talking about having memory issues. To start with, we figured it was a bit of old age blather; however, the more we saw him, the more I intuited that it could be the beginning of something more worrying.

Michael and I decided it would be good to go away for a few days, just the two of us, to enjoy being a couple and try to forget about our latest baby disappointment; forget about work, about children and family; to enjoy personal and private space; forget about having sex to get pregnant or sex with the baby monitor on in our room. We looked at where we could go in the middle of winter: anywhere far away, hot, and sunny would do for me, but Michael burns after five minutes in the sun. In the end, we decided to go to Rome. I had been there before and loved it. Besides, we would be much nearer home than the Caribbean if Victoria needed us and we had to fly back earlier. We could leave Victoria with the au pair, my mother, and my aunt.

A couple of days before travelling, there was a tingling sensation in me and a sense of blossoming. Pregnancy hormones were kicking in abruptly; I experienced tiredness and confusion, obvious signs that usually accompanied my pregnancies. It had been six weeks since my last miscarriage, and I seemed to get pregnant with the click of a finger. We were not trying for a pregnancy yet. Nevertheless, I went to the supermarket, where I spent about £30 on three pregnancy tests from different brands. One positive test. Two positive tests. Three positive tests.

It was as clear as water that I was pregnant. I had all the symptoms. Common sense went out of the window. Pregnancy madness came back, together with ardent planning, anxieties, and the happiness of what was yet to come. The injections and progesterone were back too, taking away any hope of an enjoyable and relaxing time off. Instantly, it was all about counting dates, looking at my underwear for any discharge or blood, reasoning what I should do and what

I should not do. Never mind the enjoyable sex.

We still went to Italy. We had already paid for the trip, and my mum was on her way to London. By that time, we had booked the time off work. Flying at such an early stage of pregnancy should be fine. We left Victoria at home with my mother and Evelina.

Rome is a beautiful city with great places to eat, but I didn't want to have any wine with our food. Italians do not take *no wine* for an answer lightly, so we told everybody I was pregnant. We enjoyed the freedom of talking about it at such an early stage; since we were away from our home environment it didn't matter. Italians love children. We were asked lots of questions and congratulated on the happy news. We had no sex in case it could damage the pregnancy. During my last pregnancy, I had rubbed my skin with ice before having an injection, as I find it less painful if the skin is cold; so every night, we asked for a bucket of ice. Sure, the hotel staff speculated that we were having a wild time in our room. I spent my time walking on eggshells, wondering whether I should have a look in the trendy stores or focus on maternity shops.

Needing a rest because of the pregnancy was a good excuse for me not to visit the Vatican. Michael was keen on seeing Michelangelo's Sistine Chapel. While he visited it, I stayed at the hotel. We had a fantastic room, and just being there, enjoying the space and facilities, was fabulous. Michael enjoyed his solo excursion. He suspected the real reason why

I didn't accompany him was because I am a true agnostic and my fifteen years in a school run by nuns brings me memories I'd rather leave behind.

I had been reading articles about meditation for a few months and had bought a couple of books and CDs about how to practise it. If meditation helped me to keep calm, it was a great thing for me to try. Michael was sceptical about any New Age solutions or natural medicine; he laughed at the idea.

I practised my meditation. I visualised the baby growing in my belly every day. I hugged the baby. I welcomed the heat of the baby inside my belly, my whole body warming up to him. I could visualise the face, the little hands, the eyes of the baby gazing at me intensely. The strong connection with this baby was amazing. My baby. I enjoyed the good vibes. I loved being pregnant, planned or unplanned; who cared if it worked this time? I could see my body glowing, getting stronger, and developing to nurture the pregnancy. It was all sacred and intensely warm.

I told Michael how foolish he was – he was not even prepared to give meditation a try. I declared it was the greatest discovery of my life.

We came back home after five days, on a Saturday morning. I went to the supermarket to buy two new pregnancy tests. I wanted to see the positive result again because I had my doubts; it was all happening so swiftly after my last operation. As much as I wanted it and I sensed my baby growing in me, at the back of my mind, it was too good to be true. I didn't understand how I could be pregnant that easily; my body was still in pain, unrecovered since the Christmas miscarriage.

I tried the first test: negative. The second one: negative.

How foolish I felt. All those injections. The holiday wasted, and because I'd taken those days off, I had then even fewer days left to use to rest for a future pregnancy or to take care of Victoria if there was an emergency. Though the lowest point of all was my attempts at meditation, hugging my baby, and those visions of the baby inside my body and our mutual endless love for each other. On one hand, I can see how powerful this visualisation technique can be; on the other hand, I have first-hand experience of how mistaken it can be. I could convince myself I am the Queen of England, and then what?

Michael had made his point too.

Dr More and her three phones

We were left without solutions after the third miscarriage and feeling quite imbecilic about the imagined pregnancy. We could not be sure about anything. We had lost an apparently healthy baby when we had followed the doctors' advice, despite doing exactly as we had done in the past with Victoria – minus the acupuncture.

I was referred to the lupus clinic for further advice. I had questions I wanted answering.

Professor Beverley Hunt at the lupus clinic at St Thomas' had been great when I had met her previously. After our meeting, she had sent a letter confirming that I should follow the same treatment I had with Victoria for the first twelve weeks of a future pregnancy. Professor Hunt also confirmed in writing that I did not have APS.

I wanted to talk to her again about what we should do next; we needed something extra to pull a rabbit out of the magician's hat. At the back of my mind was not only my last miscarriage but the fact that I had nearly lost Victoria too, and Kylie was not around to help. I trusted Professor Hunt's knowledge.

Unfortunately, not only at St Thomas' but in all hospitals, you typically do not get to see the head of department. I had originally only met Professor Hunt because the medical student with whom I'd had my maternity clinic appointment had wanted to double-check everything with her before giving me any advice, so eventually she'd ended up coming along. That had been a piece of top-notch luck.

While I was waiting in the corridor for my first appointment in the lupus clinic, I could not help listening to the large number of people arriving at the department who were fighting to get an appointment with Professor Hunt rather than with the other two doctors who worked there. 'We are all the same here,' they were told. 'We speak together about each case at the end of the day, so you will be fine.'

One of these two doctors who nobody wanted to have an appointment with was Dr More, and I was seeing her that day. I kept an open mind about it. If she was half as good as her boss and double-checked things with her in case of doubt, it would be more than enough. Dr More – who was also pregnant – knew everything. Before we started our meeting, she told me she had been left in charge of three mobiles from other departments of the hospital because they were short of staff. She was sorry, but she had to keep an eye on them. Fair enough, I appreciated that. If there was an emergency and she had to run to another department, so be it.

However, we had a fifteen-minute appointment, during which the phones rang continuously. We never talked for more than thirty or forty seconds without being interrupted. I found this frustrating, but it was not my main irritation. I tried to have a conversation about why the treatment had not worked twice, since it hadn't stopped the bleeding when I was pregnant with Victoria and this last time, when I had lost a healthy baby. It was not about having an argument; I was looking for a new lead and a new approach in order to seek assurances for a future pregnancy. I was told there was nothing else to try or investigate: the treatment is effective, I was told. It works all the time.

She told me I needed to have the injections, progesterone, and aspirin for twenty weeks as standard. I had a letter signed by her boss stating it was twelve weeks, as well as confirmation from St Thomas' (during the previous pregnancy), and from Spain that the treatment should only go on until week twelve. She told me that everybody was wrong, including her boss and her colleagues in the lupus department and the pregnancy unit at St Thomas', her hospital: it should be until week twenty. I politely highlighted that everybody else seemed not only to suggest something different but everybody else agreed on it. Not a chance; they were all wrong. The phone rang one more time. It was impossible to have a conversation. I gave up. Nobody is that clever that they can see patients while answering three mobiles at the same time.

I left fuming. I wrote a letter of complaint that I never sent, being painfully complaint-shy. It is not good to keep your anger inside. It kills your soul.

I had two further meetings at the lupus clinic in the following year, in both cases with the other doctor. She was a sympathetic person, but again I left disheartened. Every single question I asked was met with: 'I don't know, I need to double-check with Professor Hunt. We all have regular meetings here. I'll write you a letter with the advice to follow.' I did not receive any letters.

MISCARRIAGE NUMBER FOUR
Work–Life Balance

There were many reasons why I kept trying for another baby. I have always been afraid of loneliness. I like the idea of big families and Victorian Christmas dinners. I did not want my daughter to grow up as an only child. When I looked at how close my grandmother was to her two sisters and how much they loved each other, they could not have been luckier. My grandmother's last word before she died was her sister's name. My mother and her sister are also close; they support each other. They live together now, along with their brother, who – like my aunt – never got married. It is fabulous to see how they help each other out and always have a good laugh, in between their bickering and the *I know better than you* routine. I didn't have a sister, and I spent my childhood hoping for one, my friend for life. I ended up with two younger brothers. They spent sixteen years hitting each other and breaking one another's toys. They have a better, calmer relationship now that they are older.

True, I could fall pregnant with a boy. I expected more sport activities and lots of talk about cars, if he followed my own brother's preferences. Happy to do any activity anyway with a girl or a boy. I would have signed on the dotted line without hesitation for a healthy boy.

There was also one powerful reason to keep on trying, which my multiple miscarriages had finally made me understand. Formerly, when I had read headlines such as, 'couple get first child after eighteen unsuccessful pregnancies', I had been judgmental: 'Why on earth would you keep trying? Why would you not accept it and move on?' It was clear, after my own experiences, that the only one way to cope with a miscarriage was to succeed, to have a child, and, in that in a way, mend the sorrow of previous failures.

By March, I was merrily pregnant again. Every time a new pregnancy commenced, I was full of joy, grateful that getting pregnant was quick and easy. Each time, along with the happiness, came an increasing fear of losing the baby. I calculated the due date first, then immediately marked on my calendar when it was going to be around week eight to twelve, to make sure I didn't book any activities or holidays in case I needed to go to hospital.

This time, I convinced myself it was going to work. Why did I expect success after all the previous disappointments? Purely because I had no option. I could not allow myself to consider anything else; I did not believe I could be that unlucky. There was no new science, no new treatments that I could try. Nonetheless, the message coming from the medical sector was to keep on trying: 'It might work next time'; that is what I needed to believe. I had a healthy daughter. There was, therefore, no reason to fear that I could not carry a pregnancy safely until birth.

My new baby was due in December, on my birthday – what were the odds of this happening? I would have loved it.

If you want an abortion, you can get help – but if you have a miscarriage …?

When I told the GP that I was pregnant, his first question was: 'Are you happy about that? There are things we can do.' I could not have been happier about my pregnancy, but I was dismayed about his response. I went to the surgery to share the good news (and get my medicines), but unfortunately, the GP's reaction was to let me know about termination opportunities.

I left with the bitter taste that if a pregnant woman wanted a termination, there was more help available and more facilities than for a woman losing a wanted child. A woman who requests an abortion can also have an operation; however, a woman who is miscarrying is told, in some hospitals, to go home and take it easy. This seemed unfair to me. I have seen adverts in newspapers and magazines offering 'a termination during your lunch hour'.

Early scans were fine. I started on the medication again. I did not imagine for a second that the treatment was any guarantee of success. Michael still believed it was what we needed to do. I hated the distressing injections. The progesterone was difficult too, as within days I was an enormous blooming balloon. It made me tired, and it was difficult to hide that I was pregnant when I wanted to keep the news quiet.

Perhaps every time I started a new pregnancy, I underestimated the baggage I carried with me. My body may not have been feeling its best. More worryingly, I was neglecting my mind, which was cracking under the pressure. My brain never rested. The doctors were adamant there was nothing else they could check from a medical point of view; however, if I didn't have APS, it had to be *something else*, and I was not on the right treatment for this *something else*, whatever it was. At the time, there had been alarming headlines in the press: an aspirin a day is not worth the risk of death. And I was not just taking aspirin.

Furthermore, I unequivocally did not look forward to meeting the midwives again. But it was the price I had to pay to have a baby. I needed to get on with the whole pregnancy package. My doubts were giving me too much anguish. I could get no mental peace. I was a little mouse spinning on a wheel to nowhere.

I was no longer having acupuncture. Kylie had gone to India, and I didn't have time to look for a new acupuncturist, not to mention go to appointments. I was the only one who believed acupuncture had played a part in Victoria's pregnancy. Each time I mentioned it to anybody, I received funny looks.

I was keeping my head down at work. Since my last pregnancy had failed, my plan of taking one day a week as holiday until August was no longer an option. I was still allowed to work one day a week from home for the time being. I must confess I probably did no more than an hour's work on those days. Not because I didn't want to. It was impossible since I was at home alone with a toddler all day long, and she was not taking *not now* for an answer. I kept an eye on emails and replied to the urgent ones right away. That was it. I tried to make up for it by working at night when Victoria went to bed and on the train on my way to the office the next day. Evelina needed time off and always escaped from the house when I was there.

Evelina had been marvellous to us in every possible way. I remember one summer day when we hosted a barbecue for friends, and we told her she could invite some friends too. Towards the end of the day, she told me she was going for a night out with her friends. However, before leaving, the girls cleaned the whole kitchen. When I went back inside the house, there was not a single plate for me to wash. Victoria loved her unconditionally. I used to find it hard at dinner time when Victoria preferred to sit in Evelina's arms rather than with me after my long day at work. Victoria would also rather spend time with Evelina than with my mother, and there were a few issues when my mother was here with Evelina.

Since Christmas, Evelina's hours had increased. She had also split up with her Swedish boyfriend, who had given her a 'come back to Sweden and live with me' ultimatum. One day, out of the blue, she told me she was bored with her job. Since

I had been back at work, she had found her days were too long and isolated. She wanted to stop being an au pair and look for a job in a clothes shop, where she could talk to young people like her.

I cried that night. Evelina was fantastic, and I loved her. It was a bitter blow that she wanted to leave. Au pairs usually stay for a maximum of twelve months, which was looming on the horizon. I had hoped she would be willing to stay for longer since she had decided she didn't want to study at university and didn't have any other real plans for the future. Evelina said she was prepared to stay with us until we could find somebody else. She didn't know I was pregnant. We remain in contact with her, and she has babysat for us on numerous occasions. Today, she works as a nanny, as she is fantastic with children.

We needed a new au pair straightaway and contacted the same agency we had used when Evelina came to us. It took a few weeks to find somebody; it was the wrong time of the year, we were told. At last, we decided on a new Swedish girl. Evelina had found a job at a clothes shop and moved out to give her the room. The new girl, Pia, arrived on a Thursday night. The next morning, Pia got up and told me she wanted to leave. She explained her sister was the one who wanted her to be an au pair in London. It sounded exciting to be in a big city for a year – that is, it sounded exciting to the married, older sister, but not to our au pair. Pia liked small, quiet cities and she missed her dog, who she had left at her alcoholic mother's home because her dad, who she lived with, worked full-time and had some health issues, which meant he couldn't take care of her pet.

Pia was a nice girl. Victoria liked her, and I was confident she could do the job, so I asked Evelina to show Pia around London to see if she would change her mind. (I never told her I was pregnant.) After two days of sightseeing, Pia concluded that she hated London; it was far too busy for her taste. She could not cope with the trains, the tube, and the crowds. She did not want to disappoint her family by going back home; that was her main worry. I told her she should do what was best for in life her, not for others, and she had a dog waiting for her in Sweden anyway.

Pia didn't waste a second. After letting me know, she went to her room and booked a plane ticket for early the next morning – I had told her she didn't need to work her two weeks' notice. A year later, I received an email from her apologising. I told her there was nothing to apologise for and I hoped she was doing something she enjoyed.

Fortunately, my mother and aunt were on their way over from Spain to see their granddaughter and could stay for two weeks. We found some (free) childcare there. Victoria was a year and a half; there was no nice Evelina, so relatives would have to do. I didn't tell them I was pregnant either; I could imagine my mother climbing the wall in anger at me for continuing to try for another baby.

At week eight I started bleeding again. Michael and I

went to the Early Pregnancy Unit at St Thomas' together. We met another young doctor and were told again that it was happening because of my age. We had to wait for an ultrasound scan. It was, as always, a busy place, with many couples sitting together looking nervous. Nobody was talking much.

By the time we had the scan, the bleeding had stopped. We and the technician could hear a heartbeat on the monitor – just like it had happened in Victoria's case. We were euphoric. The technician looked relieved and very pleased for us.

Afterwards, we talked to a nurse. She was extremely glad for us. 'It was just a false alarm. It can happen in the first three months of the pregnancy – bleeding does not always mean the pregnancy has failed,' the nurse told us. I remembered a few months back, when one of my brothers and his wife, who was ten weeks pregnant, drove for five hours to see us in Spain to help us with our wedding menu, she had started bleeding. They went to hospital, where she was told it was presumably caused by the long car trip. She went on to have a girl.

We knew this little one was a fighter like our daughter and were sure the baby would manage to pull through. We were winning. Michael and I hugged when we came out of the Early Pregnancy Unit. 'This baby is as strong as Victoria,' we said, convinced we were going to have a relatively calm pregnancy, as we had with our daughter. Michael went to his office straight from the hospital, while I went back home.

I told my mother about the pregnancy and the hospital visit when I arrived home. She was not pleased. 'You should not be trying for another baby after your history of miscarriages,' she said.

We contacted the agency to get a replacement for Pia. Still the wrong time of the year. There was only one girl wanting to come to London, so she would have to do.

She arrived when my mother and aunt left. I took some of my precious time off to get to know her and explain the daily routine. My daughter did not like her at all. She would run away from her, which I found odd since she' liked every other single person she met – although she had her favourites. The au pair, a 25-year-old Swedish girl, didn't seem to be interested in either children or children's activities. I took her along to children's music and dancing lessons, for her to learn how to get there and what to do. She looked bored, totally disengaged. She said she thought London was dirty and dangerous, and she still had not decided whether she wanted to be an au pair – I had assumed she had made up her mind before landing in the country. I didn't like her.

I saw Victoria was scared of her. I only left them together on two occasions when I needed to go out. Afterwards, I noticed Victoria slapping herself when she did something 'wrong', such as dropping an item on the floor or throwing toys, which led me to believe that the au pair was hitting my child. The au pair told me that in the past she had only taken care of relatives' children and that it was different when you were with a child that you loved because they were part of your family.

One day, I was unable to go out because Victoria was hysterically crying and didn't want to be left alone with her. I went back to the nursery room, where I saw the au pair handling her roughly as if they were both fighting. I decided I could not leave the house, so I stayed playing with Victoria to calm her down. While I was thinking that I had to get rid of the au pair as soon as possible, the girl came to the nursery crying and said she had just read an email from her grandmother, telling her that her dad was unwell and depressed. I told her to go back home at once, since she was needed by her family in Sweden. Again, I kept my pregnancy to myself. I found it progressively difficult to work out how I was going to juggle my life, work, baby, pregnancy, and childcare. I was running fast with no clear direction.

Michael had been telling me for around a year now that I did not need to work. We could afford for me to stay at home. It would be nice if I could take care of Victoria myself. Friends and family kept telling me I needed to take it easy for a pregnancy to succeed. Michael's mum had many miscarriages before having him. When she got pregnant with him, she'd decided to put her feet up for nine months and do nothing but lay on the sofa reading Charles Dickens' novels. It didn't sound like a bad plan. I liked Dickens too.

Nevertheless, I clung on to my work. I remembered with sorrow my mother's miserable marriage; if she had not held on to her job, she would now be a battered stay-at-home wife, rather than a sparkling, free woman enjoying her single life and pension. Not that Michael was anything similar to my father, but I grew up too close to danger and learnt to fear a lack of independence. It wasn't a fear based on something that had happened to other people in the news or in the movies; it was based on personal experience. I had worked extremely hard to be where I was and was very proud of myself. I had plans and dreams. When a friend, single and yearning for a baby, asked me if having a baby was the fulfilment of my life, the answer came without a doubt. No. Becoming a mother was a wonderful gift; however, the so-called fulfilment of my life would come with career success.

One night not long after our positive scan, I was sitting on my side of the bed, tired and nervous about whether I would see any more bleeding. 'You don't need to work if you don't want to,' Michael suggested one more time. It would be best for my pregnancy. The baby had survived the bleeding, so was I willing to risk his or her life?

In that moment, I decided to stop working since we had no childcare anyway. My pregnancy was worth fighting for. Not that my previous pregnancies weren't. However, maybe putting my feet up and forgetting about the stress of work could help the baby, as well as make my body and mind stronger. I asked to be signed off sick; that way I didn't need to work my notice. I could take it easy at home and we could cope with not having childcare.

I remembered my supervisor in one of my first jobs in London. Alice, my boss, had called me at work one day. It was her birthday, so I presumed she was running late. She told me she was pregnant; however, a miscarriage had started that morning. She didn't want anybody to know. She hadn't told anyone at work she was pregnant, and it was news for me too. She asked me to let everybody know she was unwell, without giving details. The whole day long, people kept coming into our office and telling me how cheeky it was of her to throw a sickie on her birthday. Weeks later, she told me she had suffered many miscarriages. She had an investigation done and received the devastating news that she would never be able to have children. Doctors could not find a reason for the miscarriages; still, she was told to forget about them.

Alice had never enjoyed working in our company. After the devastating news, she decided to quit to become a foster mum. A month later, she was gone. She started her new life with a long cruise to the Caribbean. She believed she was seasick when coming back to England on the ship. As it happened, Alice was suffering from pregnancy sickness; a few months later, she went on to have a baby girl. She was sure it had all worked out well because she wasn't working. It could be what I needed too.

I had no alternative options on offer. It was best for Victoria and my new baby. I had to put them first. I told myself it was only a temporary situation anyway. Working full-time, having to ask for time off constantly, missing workdays, making fake excuses, when really, I was having to run to hospital or recover from operations, was making things difficult for me in the office. I was giving my colleagues the impression that I was unreliable and that I could not focus on my job. I didn't like looking unprofessional. Ideally, I liked to keep my personal life to myself at work.

On the positive side, Victoria's behaviour improved dramatically. After only a few days of me being at home, she became so calm, clearly happier than when I was working.

Two weeks later, the bleeding started again. This time, it looked thicker, more persistent. I had no doubt what was coming. I went back to St Thomas' to the Early Pregnancy Unit. This time, I went on my own, as Michael could not make it out of work. Although we had no au pair, Evelina was delighted to babysit as she was free and looking to move jobs.

The kingdom of white men

I desperately needed to know whether there was still a heartbeat. I met a nurse when I arrived, rather than a doctor, and was offered a blood test to check my iron levels. The nurse added that she could examine my vagina to see if I was still bleeding. Neither of those options would give me any clue as to the health of the baby. I'd had many blood tests in the past to check my iron levels. They had always been – surprisingly – fine. Sadly, I was able to tell her I was still bleeding without the need for any examinations.

I was told I could not have an ultrasound scan unless I had an appointment. That was new. It had not been the case before – even if I had waited there for hours. What was different this time? I got upset and frustrated. I was scared and jittery. I needed to know whether there was still a heartbeat, if my baby was still alive, for God's sake – what did I care about my iron levels? I was told it was impossible for them to do a scan without an appointment. I would have to come back.

I was given an appointment for two days later, the earliest they could offer me. Michael said he would try to join me there if he could. I duly returned after over forty-eight hours of agonised waiting, without any fresh bleeding, to be told: 'Sorry, we made a mistake in our appointment book and you will have to come back again tomorrow.' They accepted that the nurse I had spoken to previously had filled in the correct paperwork for me to have a scan on that date and I also had a letter printed by them on the day to confirm my appointment. However, when somebody manually filled in the appointment slots at the reception desk, she had written down my appointment on the wrong day.

I wanted to throw myself on the floor and cry. I begged them to see me; I explained how cruel the situation was for me. 'No,' they repeated. 'If we could do anything to fit you in, we would, but it is absolutely impossible for us to offer you a scan today. You need to come back tomorrow.' I didn't have the will or the mental and physical capacity to continue arguing any more.

On my way out of hospital, I met Michael coming in. I told him that we had no chance of a scan, because they had made a mistake in their appointment book, and I had already begged for one. My husband, with his Oxford-educated English accent and his blue eyes, went to talk to the same two women I had been talking to; he told them that the situation was unacceptable. Within the next ten minutes, I had my two-minute-long ultrasound scan and my bad news. Knowing earlier would not have saved the baby; however, it would have helped my mental state and general health.

Indeed, depending on who was asking, it seemed it *was* possible to get an appointment on the same day, as it had happened before when I had gone there with my husband. The experience made me feel like garbage – voiceless and easily ignored when there was no man with me.

This situation reminded me of a similar case years earlier, when a female neighbour and I had tried for a year to get a satellite dish installed on the roof of the building to be able to watch cable TV. Fed up with waiting and endless excuses, my neighbour asked her husband to get involved. The following day, her husband contacted the company that was meant to do the work. He made a real fuss; within less than twenty-four hours, they came and put the dish up. Why? What is wrong with a polite woman with a strong argument asking for something to be done?

The good ERPC

I requested an ERPC/SMM when the miscarriage was confirmed. No emergency lists for me this time – I was getting the hang of it. I explained I wanted to be on the day surgery list and was given an appointment for two weeks later.

This was my second ERPC on the NHS at St Thomas' – before I found out that our private health insurance would cover it. During the two weeks of waiting, I was in no pain. There was no bleeding or discharge. I could have believed I was blissfully pregnant, if I had not known. After I had my first ERPC there, I had been in pain for three months, so I was a bit wary about the aftermath of the procedure.

As on the previous occasion, I arrived early in the morning. Since I now knew the routine, this time I brought a book with me to have something to distract me. I stated that I wanted to keep it and didn't mind if it got lost.

I had a preliminary conversation with a doctor, as everybody there did. He had my folder in his hands and started talking to me about my details. Everything seemed to be incorrect, from how many weeks pregnant I was, to the side of the uterus where the foetus was, to when I'd found out I was pregnant. He told me about a scan that I had supposedly gone to when I had not even been pregnant. It seemed clear that, although he had my folder, the papers inside belonged to somebody else; there had been a mix-up. This troubled me, and he looked confused too. He sent me to the toilet to take a pregnancy test – as an excuse for him to make some calls. As a joke, I clarified that I was there for an ERPC, not for a leg to be amputated, thinking of the occasional weird news about people getting the wrong operation done by mistake . Better safe than sorry.

I did not meet the surgeon who was going to do the procedure. When I woke up after my operation, the doctor with whom I had spoken earlier came to my bedside to tell me, 'Oh, you were so lucky – the senior surgeon did your operation today.' I did not have any pain, any problems, or bleeding afterwards. I wondered who had done my first operation.

We requested an analysis of the foetus. We had to fight again for this to be done since, although this was my fourth miscarriage, I'd had two sets of two consecutive miscarriages – not three in a row; it was still officially considered an 'unlucky' pregnancy. We found out after the tests that this baby had Down's Syndrome. It gave rise to a confused mixture of emotions: the sadness of losing another baby, the fear of something being wrong with our DNA, the concern about my age – which was thirty-eight at the time.

After this new heartbreak, I had to go back to my old company to collect my things and attend a small gathering in my department to say goodbye to my colleagues. I took Victoria with me to make it quick. I was not in the right frame of mind for long lunches. However, I appreciated the fact that some of the women were keen to see my daughter. Not everybody had been told I had miscarried the latest baby. I had people coming to me to offer their congratulations on the new pregnancy and wishing me good luck.

Discovering gardening

I was at home, not working anymore and feeling rather down. A week earlier, I had taken delivery of two apple trees I had bought online. After a cold winter, we had a large empty space in the garden where many plants had died. During Victoria's pregnancy. I had been reading again, this time in English, my beloved *Famous Five* series. In the books, the children were often sent to the bottom of the garden to collect fruit for cakes and salad for tea. The books got me thinking I wanted to do the same.

I had been disappointed when I first saw the trees. They looked like dry, thin sticks with tiny dry roots. Not even long or strong enough to be a walking stick. I had left them in a semi-open box in the living-room since their arrival. I was not sure whether there was any point in planting them outside. Now I was sat on the sofa, a metre away from them, when out of nowhere I looked at the box one more time and I said to myself, *I cannot save my babies, but I am going to save these trees from dying.*

I commenced what I figured would be ten minutes of light work in the garden, digging up a couple of holes. After two hours of energetic work, removing large roots of dead plants and planting the new trees, I felt fulfilled and strangely calm. The exhausting physical activity made me forget about my sadness, along with everything else that was going on. Both trees have grown healthily, and we get tasty apples every summer. I have been a keen gardener since then. I find it calming.

MISCARRIAGE NUMBER FIVE
Great Expectations

In November, our strength returned once more; somehow, despite our disappointment in June, we wanted to try again and give Victoria a sibling. I had serious doubts as to whether it was ever going to work for us. Four times 'unlucky' and the extra complication of Down's Syndrome with the last baby were not uplifting facts. My head was once again spinning with thoughts, day and night.

I was at home full-time. We had a great new au pair who helped me a lot with Victoria. It had taken us five months to find Malin. Incredibly, the agency had offered us an epileptic girl to take care of a two-year-old, who would be unable to help if she suffered a bad seizure, a girl from an Eastern European country who wanted to bring her mum along, and a girl who had started an au pair placement in the USA and who, dreadfully, was drugged and sexually abused during a night out – she was keen on coming to London, but I sincerely believed she needed time for herself.

At long last, by August, we managed to get Malin, another Swedish national. She was mature and kind. Her mother had been working as a foster carer since she had been a young girl, so Malin was used to children in her busy household. She told us that at one point there were ten children in her home, including herself and her two siblings. I should have appreciated her more at the time; I was so upset about not working that I didn't give her enough credit for all she did (we are still in touch and are great friends now).

I could put my feet up and take it easy with a new pregnancy when it happened. I could not put my mind to rest, though. I kept looking for the ideal local-well-paid-interesting-part-time job. I was anxious about treatments, hospitals, about having arguments with midwives, about losing the baby again, about whether I should look for a new place to have acupuncture. In retrospect, I should have had some counselling.

When it was time to get down to business, I got pregnant effortlessly in the first month we tried. We had spoken before the pregnancy about not having any medical treatment. Despite that, once I told Michael I was pregnant, he denied that any conversation about not having treatment had ever taken place.

He believed he had found the solution to the problem. He wanted us to go back to Mr Mackay, who was his preferred choice. We started seeing him again, privately. Michael was adamant that I had to use the brand of injections Mr Mackay had given us the first time, rather than the brand we'd had from St Thomas'. Both Mr Mackay and St Thomas' Hospital had categorically told us in the past that there was no difference between the brands. They were precisely the same. However, we all needed to believe in something, and Michael believed that was going to make a difference.

I tried to be positive, to get on with the idea of the treatment. But I could not. It was making me angry and paranoid. I kept checking my underwear for blood about a hundred times a day. I told myself repeatedly this time was going to be the last time I was pregnant, independent of the result.

We went for a scan in week six. There was a heartbeat. We were ecstatic. We were more hopeful – after hearing the heartbeat and not having any discharge – that it was going to work for us. What is there left if you lose your hope against hope? I decided it was a girl. Her name was going to be Elizabeth. My little queen Elizabeth.

The next two weeks passed in bliss with no problems, no discharge, nothing to report except extremely bad nausea. I had been lucky when it came to nausea in the past – if nothing else – in all my pregnancies. I did not suffer any of the common pregnancy symptoms that most women have. On this occasion, I was sick twenty-four hours a day, every day.

Kylie, when she was still living in London, had recommended that if I ever experienced pregnancy nausea, I should put a piece of lemon under my tongue, which proved to be an outstanding remedy. Although, in normal circumstances, I could not have put a piece of lemon in my mouth – I find it far too bitter – it didn't bother me when I was pregnant. I couldn't taste it, yet it stopped the sickness every time after only a couple of minutes. I was encouraged by this sickness; maybe it meant I was having a normal pregnancy with harmless discomfort for a change.

We went back for a scan in week eight. Doctors call them reassurance scans: nothing is wrong, but they keep anxious parents calm when they can have a look to check the pregnancy development. We had kept a scan of Victoria from the same week. We wondered how this baby was going to look at the same stage.

We arrived at the private hospital in Wimbledon to see Mr Mackay and to have an ultrasound scan around eight a.m. on the Saturday morning. We were seeing him privately at a cost of £250 for a fifteen-minute appointment. I do not have the stomach to be a doctor, but if I had, I would happily work on early Saturday mornings.

His technician came into the office, a pleasant woman whom we already knew from previous visits. We talked to Mr Mackay too. We had no concerns about the pregnancy. We all were joyful.

I went behind the curtains and got ready to lay on the examination table. The technician came along, while Michael and the doctor had a friendly chat. To start with, the ultrasound monitor always faces the technician only, not the patient.

She said nothing. I saw it in her eyes.

She became agitated, still saying nothing, but I knew. She started to move the ultrasound transducer across my body, left and right. She called Mr Mackay. Both looked at the screen together. Still no word to me. I could not believe it was happening again.

He had to tell us: the baby was gone. There was not a heartbeat. It had not developed since our last scan two weeks earlier.

I was numb with grief, almost detached from the situation. I was not there, I was a mere spectator observing a scene on a screen. I could switch the screen off, leave the scene at any time to continue with my life. Sometimes life is too cruel to feel anything else.

We needed to book a new ERPC. Mr Mackay and Michael wanted me to have the ERPC there. I disagreed. I was adamant that I preferred to have it done at St Thomas' in order to try to get an investigation carried out there instead. I had (at last!) reached the notorious three consecutive miscarriages.

However, Mr Mackay believed firmly in the treatment he'd recommended for me – and nothing would change his mind. He was not open to other ideas, treatments, or research possibilities – even if science still needed to catch up with new developments. I did not understand how he could still claim that mine was the right treatment. How many times do you need to hit your head against a wall to know it hurts? Mr Mackay had been Michael's choice. He was a caring person with a real interest in women's issues. In spite of this, I disagreed with his theory. Another reason not to want to do any further tests in his clinic was that we had already done them there. While I had no concerns about their professionalism, I was eager to get a fresh pair of eyes on the matter.

We left the hospital soon afterwards, strangely calm. It was a calm tempered by sorrow – and failure. A sad end to my pregnancy quest, but at least it had ended; no more injections. More significant, no more dead babies.

After leaving the hospital, we went for breakfast at the nearby Le Pain Quotidian in Wimbledon Village, one of my favourites. I didn't fancy anything from the menu, although now that I wasn't pregnant, I was allowed to eat anything I liked. It sank in then that I was never going to have two children. I had lost my future, and I had no idea why.

We sat there trying to make pleasant conversation, as if life was all right. We both agreed that this was the last time we would try to have another baby. It was time to move on, to find of something else to occupy our lives with. I glanced around the café. Everybody else having breakfast was also coupled off, but every other couple in the cafe had two children with them. I looked at them in misery.

I went to the Early Pregnancy Unit at St Thomas' two days later. They had sent me a letter for an appointment regarding my previous miscarriage in June. I had it in mind that it was an appointment to check on my current pregnancy, and there was a bit of confusion when I arrived. Nevertheless, they confirmed the miscarriage. I was taken to a quiet room to talk about my next ERPC. It was such a nice little room with the sun coming in through a large window, a beautiful view of the Thames and all the famous buildings along the river. I felt out of place; that room should be a place for good news, not for me.

Casually, the nurse asked whether I had any health insurance. I answered that, yes, we did, but health insurers do not want to know anything about pregnancies. The nurse said we should double-check with our insurance company because many of them would cover ERPCs since, at this point, the woman is not pregnant anymore; the ERPC is considered to be an operation concerning the health of the person. This was fantastic news in the circumstances because it could be done much quicker. Maybe I could avoid the two weeks' waiting? Why had nobody ever mentioned this before?

Dr Hamilton

The nurse asked me to sit outside while I waited for a doctor who dealt with private operations to organise my appointment. I hoped I could get an early appointment. I called Michael at work to ask him to check the situation with our insurance company and to get an authorisation number from them.

Michael called me back quickly: our private insurance undoubtedly covered ERPCs. As the nurse had disclosed, once it is established that the pregnancy is not viable, the main focus is to treat the individual who needs an operation to improve her health. How foolish that we had never realised that. We had read the terms and conditions of our insurance carefully; we assumed an ERPC was a pregnancy-related operation.

Dr Judith Hamilton appeared within a few minutes. I liked her from start. She looked interested, proactive, and knowledgeable. She listened to our summary – rant – of our five miscarriages and the treatments: my despair at not getting enough ultrasound scans, waiting for operations, and young doctors telling me I was too old for this. She checked her diary and the operation theatre timetable. She gave me an appointment for two days later.

This time, it took place at Guy's Nuffield House; a private hospital and a small building, quiet and calm. I was given a time, and I did not have to do much waiting. All went well, and we left right away after being given the okay.

Different miscarriage, different reaction

My favourite colour is red, beautiful, dark red. After my first miscarriage, and the sight of those dark shades of red blood coming out, I could not face anything red, from a dress to a pen. Coming across a red item would send me into a panic, remembering the miscarriage. This reaction lasted for about five years before ultimately fading away. It took me about six years to buy a new red dress. I did not suffer this way with any other miscarriage. They each manifested in a different way. In one case, I had bad insomnia; in another case, terrible constipation.

My head refused to believe it had happened once again with the latest miscarriage. I remember crossing Westminster Bridge towards St Thomas' and looking at the river, feeling joyful because I was going for a maternity appointment. I had to stop walking to think hard about whether I really had a pregnancy appointment or whether I was on my way for some tests prior to the latest ERPC. For weeks after it had all ended, I kept going into children's shops to choose outfits for my baby. I had these sudden moments of total confusion where I needed to make a huge effort to remember whether I was pregnant or not.

More disturbing is that on three different occasions, I had episodes of forgetting who I was, where I was, or what I was doing there. The first time, I was at the local supermarket after visiting the GP; in the blink of an eye, I didn't know who I was, where I was, why I was there. It was more dangerous when it happened when I was driving with my daughter in the car. There was a click in my mind, and afterwards, I did not know where I was, why I was driving, or where I was going.

Second investigation

I wish I had met Dr Judith Hamilton earlier on. I believe there is a strong chance we could have had a happier outcome. I found her intelligent, competent, and proactive.

After this last miscarriage, we were asked by doctors whether there was an illness or a health problem running in either family. If that had been the case, it could have helped them to pinpoint an issue with my pregnancies. As far as we knew, this was not the case. We were aware that Michael's mum had suffered at least three miscarriages before having him. Erika, when asked again, replied, 'In total, it was more than three miscarriages.' She did not want to count them.

My maternal grandmother had had a baby girl in between my mother and my aunt. This baby died when she was a few weeks old. I believe the baby died because she'd had respiratory problems. My grandmother did not talk about her ever. I decided to ask her about the baby's health problems in case it opened a new line of investigation.

What she told me was heart breaking, in a way that I had never expected. My grandparents were living in a small town without a hospital in the early 1950s. One night, the baby was feeling sick. I am not sure how old the baby was exactly, but only a few weeks. In the middle of the night, my grandfather borrowed a friend's motorbike; the three of them drove to the nearest city where there was a hospital.

There, they met a nun, who checked the baby; she told them, 'The baby is fine,' and added, 'It's late, it's cold outside; why don't you leave her here and you can collect her tomorrow morning?' They did as suggested. When my grandparents came back the following morning, they were told the baby had died; everything had been taken care of. They never saw her again.

When I was told this story, the scandal of the stolen

babies – in which nuns, as well as hospital staff, were heavily involved – had not yet reached the headlines in Spain. When it did, my grandmother, in her nineties, had Alzheimer's; I decided it was wrong to upset her with more questions that she might not be able to answer. Instead, I told my mother that she might have a lost sister somewhere. She did not believe the story. She told me she was sure the baby had died – my mother was two years old at the time.

Sadly, regarding my own pregnancies, nothing new was discovered. No genetic abnormality was found in either Michael or me during this second round of tests at St Thomas'. We were told that, theoretically, hundreds of genetic tests could be done on us, but without any indication or family medical condition, it was like finding a needle in a haystack. No women on my side of the family had suffered a miscarriage (aside from a cousin in my father's family who had married a heroin addict and had a second trimester miscarriage). Two women in my family did not have children; these were my unmarried aunt and a great aunt, who, when she failed to get pregnant, was told it was caused by internal issues. Whatever that meant, and how much doctors knew in the 1950s, I am not sure.

New tests – again – indicated that I did not have antiphospholipid syndrome. My fertility levels were all right. I asked whether they could do a sperm test for Michael. This had never been done; I was aware they did them at Zita West. I was told they would only do tests on men if there were conception problems – basically, if a woman cannot get pregnant. Sperm renews itself every three months; as a result, a test would not pick up on any previous quality issues (if there were any) at the time of conception.

I do not believe necessarily that the problem lay with Michael. However, in my humble opinion, it would have been a good idea to check other possibilities since we were repeating tests on the woman but not starting tests on the man. If we continue doing the same check-ups on a woman and don't get any wiser with the results, wouldn't it be good to try an alternative test? A reassurance test?

I had all my meetings with Dr Hamilton – once I found somebody good, I was not going to let her go; it was worth paying for her time. She led a clinic specialising in miscarriage and other fertility, early pregnancy, and women's medical issues. I did ask her if she knew the sex of the lost babies and whether something had come out after the investigation of the last miscarriage – a friend of mine had been telling me about another friend of hers who seemed to miscarry boys and had successful pregnancies when carrying girls.

Dr Hamilton told me she had the information. She asked me whether I was sure I wanted to know. I breathed deeply and heavily before replying 'yes'. The first one was a healthy boy; the second one was a boy, who had Down's Syndrome; the third one was a girl, with a different genetic issue.

After I left the meeting, I understood why she had asked whether I was sure I wanted to know the sex of my babies.

With the new information, I could put a boy's or a girl's face on them. I could give them a name. I had my list of preferred names. It was harder to bear; I knew too much. Still, I was pleased to have asked. That's all I will ever know about them.

My little girl, my Elizabeth, had a rare genetic defect called Trisomy 13 or Patau's Syndrome. Most people have 23 pairs of chromosomes, with two copies of each pair, one inherited from the mother and one from the father. Trisomy 13 means there is an extra copy in pair 13. She would not have survived outside my body. If she had been born, she would have died most probably within hours. Some babies survive a bit longer, although 90 percent die within a year of birth. Their range of intellectual disabilities and physical abnormalities is enormous, and they can suffer severely until they pass away. Most cases of Trisomy 13 are not inherited from the parents. They are a result of random events during the fusion of the egg and the sperm. Months later, when I had the strength, I researched Trisomy 13 issues. I came across some heart-breaking information.

I have never cried for Elizabeth. It remains too painful.

I told Dr Hamilton that an investigation had been done on the second miscarriage in Spain. I had been told the foetus was 'all right'. She suspected no genetic tests had been performed at the time since labs had only been able to start doing them a few months earlier. The latest technological advances meant studies could be done using only a tiny piece of tissue from the foetus. In the past, a larger piece of bodily matter was needed to carry out the test; because of the small size of the foetus and the ERPC vacuuming-type of operation, it was common for the remains of the pregnancy to be too small to be tested.

I telephoned Benigno, and he confirmed that was correct. They had been able to do other types of tests, where all the results were normal, however, there was no information regarding Down's Syndrome or Trisomy 13.

Out of the five miscarriages, we now knew there was a healthy boy, a boy with Down's Syndrome, and a girl with Trisomy 13. We had no information about the first miscarriage and not much about the second. Some foetuses were on the right-hand side of my uterus, some on the left-hand side. I had the same treatment of heparin injections, aspirin, and progesterone in my last four pregnancies.

A compelling article about super-fertile women came to my attention. The term sounds good, super-fertile women, like a super-hero type of power. A super-fertile woman is somebody who gets pregnant very easily and very quickly. Potentially that could be me, since sometimes it took only one try to get pregnant when normally doctors say it is very common to try for several months before a woman gets pregnant. I believe a couple needs to try unsuccessfully for a year before a fertility study is recommended. A small UK–Dutch study by Princess Anne Hospital and the University Medical Centre, Utrecht, found a link between recurrent miscarriage and super-fertility by studying samples taken from the wombs of women who had suffered recurrent miscarriages and those with normal fertility. The wombs of the women who had suffered from recurrent miscarriages had tried to implant any embryos, unable to distinguish good quality embryos from the poor quality embryos that should have been rejected – as usually happens. Therefore, a pregnancy that has no long-term chance of survival starts, only to be miscarried a few weeks later. Could I be one of those super-fertile women? Another characteristic of this group is how easily these women get pregnant.

I also read several studies about stress and miscarriage. Some studies suggest that severe stress – not as in 'my football team lost a match' stress, although I agree that can be very nerve-racking – can cause a miscarriage, in particular in the early stages of the pregnancy. My stress levels were off the scale – I was carrying too much life baggage, most of it having nothing to do with pregnancies, at least to start with. I mentioned this several times, especially to Mr Mackay, who categorically denied that stress and miscarriage are linked. 'Look at all the animals that have babies in the wild,' he said.

I went for a private ultrasound scan with Dr Hamilton as part of the miscarriage investigation. Although she had done the ERPC on me, it had not been possible to do a scan or see the uterus accurately at that time. She wanted to check whether I definitely had a bicornuate uterus. She asked who had told me that was the case. I was puzzled about her question; I expected it was easy for the trained eye to see.

I told her Mr Mackay had been the first doctor to assert this and later Dr Peppas had confirmed that I had a bicornuate uterus during my C-section. Dr Peppas mentioned that it was easy to see when the baby was still inside me, but more difficult once the baby was out. Books say the easiest way to see whether a uterus is bicornuate is at the time of a surgical procedure, such as a C-section. I explained that Benigno had never mentioned it to me in all the years I had been treated by him.

Dr Hamilton wanted to do the ultrasound scan on me. She wanted to check the size and shape of the uterus too. Afterwards, Dr Hamilton told me I did not have a bicornuate uterus (BU); I had a septate uterus (SU). They look similar. However, there are important differences between them, as a BU cannot be operated on. It may cause problems towards the end of the pregnancy – preterm birth, cervical incompetence, late miscarriage. A SU is a uterus that has a removable longitudinal septum, and it can cause early recurrent miscarriage. There is a risk that the uterus gets damaged during procedures to remove the septum; as a consequence, the woman will not be able to carry a future pregnancy.

I was asked to weigh up the risks in my case. Dr Hamilton disclosed that several women she was treating had had the operation done and had a successful pregnancy afterwards. Though not of all them. A septate uterus is not necessarily considered a problem for every woman and explained why

Benigno never indicated there was an issue – and why he had disagreed with Mr Mackay's diagnosis but did not want to start a discussion about it.

We agreed that I should have the septum removed privately. It was a new approach; on balance, the risk was worthwhile. Soon, I was in a private hospital again, back at Guy's Nuffield House, with a drip on my hand, waiting to go into the theatre for the cartilage removal. At least I was confident I was in good hands, because Dr Hamilton was doing the operation.

Then a young man came into the room. He announced he was a junior doctor on a placement with Dr Hamilton. He had my file in his hand and said, 'I haven't read your file yet, but you're here to have an operation because you have antiphospholipid syndrome.'

'Well, actually, I do not have antiphospholipid syndrome; I am here because I need a septum to be removed from my uterus,' I said. It was a completely different matter, APS or not APS.

'Right,' he replied.

'In any case, you do not have an operation on your uterus if you have APS,' I added.

Then he opened my file and said, 'I see here you had a miscarriage not long ago, because the baby was a freak.'

'Hello! It was my baby. She had a chromosome abnormality, but I do not like for her to be called a freak.'

After that, he decided to leave.

I was flabbergasted. Everybody needs to learn. As I've mentioned, I always agreed when doctors asked me whether a student or somebody on a work placement could sit in on my appointments. However, to say 'I have not read your file' – well, read it first and talk later. *And my baby was not a freak.*

A distant cousin of mine, with top school grades, decided to study medicine. I was surprised when I found out she was not applying for the top universities. If you do not try, you do not get. When I challenged her why that was the case, she replied, 'Because those top universities don't let you see patients to start with, but at the ones I am applying to, I get to see and talk to patients from the first day.' It is jolly nice of her to presume that she can help patients from day one, but there is a good reason why the top universities make students wait (says the grumpy patient).

A new gynaecologist, who I now visit for annual check-ups in Spain after Benigno retired (it is still easier and cheaper to see a doctor in Spain), told me the removal of the septum was the right thing to do; it had increased the chances of a good pregnancy. However, my uterus still had a strange shape, rather than a balloon-style one. It was considerably smaller on the left-hand side, making a small cavity there. According to him, any baby trying to attach itself to the left side would not have had much chance of survival; this could have explained the miscarriage of the baby after I'd had Victoria, who was on the right-hand side, and, as far as we know, a healthy baby.

I had a new and final appointment at the lupus clinic

at St Thomas'. They also agreed that, if APS had been my problem, the treatment should have worked as 'it worked on well over 90 per cent of women having the treatment'. Their suggestion was that I could have the same treatment as before, plus adding steroids to the list of drugs. There was no medical evidence to believe that steroids were going to work. However, it would be the next step if I wanted to go down that route, and they did not have anything else to offer me. Michael was entirely against the idea of me being put on steroids in view of the effects on my body. My only knowledge of steroids was of bodybuilders trying to pump up their muscles at the gym. Steroids could make a pregnancy successful; on the other hand, steroids could terminate a healthy pregnancy, I read later. It was like playing Russian roulette. I was fully against the idea of having any treatment. I had this wild belief that I would like to go to a forest – once pregnant – and stay there on my own for nine months.

I feel for those women who try month after month to get pregnant and fail in their quest – the stress, the smiley face on the fertility sticks, the waiting, the pregnancy tests, and at the end, only the disappointment. It is a draining process. I remember a colleague, now with two children, telling me about the burden of fertility sticks – the boredom of doing it to get his wife pregnant, rather than 'hey, because we like it!', and the tension of waiting for two weeks for the pregnancy test, the disappointment, and then starting the cycle all over again with the ovulation sticks.

After my fifth miscarriage, I reflected on whether the failure to get pregnant is better than being able to start a new life, only to find out later that somehow you or your body is not able to keep it safe and nurture it. That was how I felt, and it was the ultimate devastating conclusion. I'd killed my baby, but I did not know why or how.

I would have rather never got pregnant (again) than have had another miscarriage.

MISCARRIAGE NUMBER SIX
Fool's Paradise

At home, old Treacle thought she had run out of luck. It had started with the appearance of the annoying baby, which was bad enough, but then her life got even worse when we had to adopt Mitza, my mother-in-law's old grumpy female cat, when Erika eventually went into a care home.

This was double treason in Treacle's eyes. A baby was a nuisance, but another cat – how dare we! Treacle stopped being in the same room with us; she looked miserable. The two cats hated each other. Both of them were equally nasty to one another, and the display of naughty tricks and hissing was epic, worthy of its own book. Treacle decided to poo on our bed, on Michael's side, when we were out as a thank-you token for bringing the new cat into our house.

Mitza had fleas – we were too busy to take her for a check-up when she came to us, and Erika had assured us that she was up to date with vet visits. In fact, she had not been to the vet for years. She passed them on to Treacle and last in line to Victoria. Without us seeing her, Treacle had rolled around on my daughter's bed. Victoria had one of those eco mattresses; we found out later that they were the perfect bed for flea eggs, as fleas prefer natural, clean products. We had to disinfect the whole house three times to get rid of all the eggs, and eventually, we had to spend three days out of the house, leaving all the windows open to get rid of the chemicals. The lesson was clear: it pays to take the animals for their regular vet appointments, never mind how busy you think you are.

A few months later, when the two cats died – both were over sixteen years old – we went to Battersea Dogs & Cats Home and brought back two kittens. No problems with children. One of them even loves children; she goes into my daughter's room when she is having a play date with friends and sits in the middle of them. Evidently, Coco does not know the meaning of danger.

My previous pregnancy was meant to be our final attempt to have a second child. Anyhow, my latest operation, combined with the fact that I was no longer going to take any drugs – doctors, myself, and Michael agreed on that – gave me the strength I needed to give it one more chance.

We had a new appointment with Dr Hamilton. She agreed with me that we did not seem to know why the miscarriages were happening; this was not unusual; many couples do not find out the cause of their miscarriages. The same treatment had not worked now on three consecutive occasions. There was no strong medical evidence – in my case – to believe that it was going to work a fourth time. The lupus clinic agreed with this.

Dr Hamilton understood my frustration as to what to do next or how to do it. My friend Francisco sent me a medical article published in *The New England Journal of Medicine* on recurrent miscarriage. The evidence and results on trials on women with recurrent miscarriage did not show any benefits in the use of anticoagulants. The decision was up to me; some women feel reassured if they are having medical treatment with all the available drugs, while other women and couples may decide they need to do something different. There was no right answer; we were still pretty much clueless.

I looked for a new acupuncturist and found a practitioner in Neal's Yard. I went to meet her before I got pregnant to let her know about my background; I asked her whether she wanted to see me again soon. She told me to visit her again after I was pregnant; hence no body pregnancy preparation like I had done with Kylie. I told her about it, but she didn't think I needed it.

On our last meeting with Dr Hamilton, we had agreed to contact her once I was pregnant. As on previous occasions, getting pregnant was not a problem. About six weeks later, I was.

I had not had a period after the operation on my womb to remove the cartilage in January. I had a coil inserted to help with the healing, which was a standard procedure. I was told that on rare occasions the coil could stop periods all together, as happened in my case. It was also uncomfortable; I was grateful when it was removed two months later in March.

Since I wanted to know when I was going to have a fertile day, but I had no period to start counting from, I started testing myself every day. On a Sunday morning, 3 April, the long-awaited smiley appeared on the fertility stick. I ran back to our room to get to work. No doubt about it: conception day was 3 April.

A few days later, when the pregnancy was confirmed, I emailed Dr Hamilton to share the happy news. I wrote in my email to her that 'we have done the *easy bit*'. I received a reply saying that the getting pregnant bit was not easy; in fact, I had done the most difficult part of the pregnancy. Dr Hamilton always repeated that. It made me smile. If only it were true – in my case.

I had an ultrasound scan that confirmed the early stages of the pregnancy and the day of conception. I was overjoyed, confident that this pregnancy was going to work.

We were keeping it quiet as usual. It was still early days when our cleaner asked me directly whether I was pregnant again.

'Why do you ask? Am I getting fat?' I said.

'No,' she replied, 'you've been rubbing your belly in circles all morning.'

We started seeing Dr Hamilton every week, privately. We discussed the conception date with her. We were sure that this was the key day for the simple fact that we had not had sex for three weeks since we had gone away to Oxford for a romantic 'day-that-we-had-first-met' anniversary. The development of the embryo confirmed the conception date, and the ultrasound scans told us the baby was on the right side of my uterus, as was Victoria – on the good side, my bigger side.

All was well; the foetus was developing properly with a sound, fast heartbeat. We had weekly images of it. Everything was growing according to the right week: brain and heart to start with, bigger bean-like appearance later, protuberances where the arms and legs were going to appear, and so forth. At the first scan, it seemed large for its age. Nothing new there; Victoria was quite large, as were both my husband and I when we were born.

After twelve weeks, we started on the NHS. I was not ready for it. I was fearful. All changed with me. I wanted to go private. But the treatment was expensive, and I was not working; it would cost anywhere from £10,000 to £15,000. It was too much money. I felt guilty about imposing that burden on Michael, who believed that, since we had done it before at St Thomas', which had a great reputation as a maternity hospital, we could go through it one more time. One last time.

Dr Hamilton told us that the senior doctor in charge of high-risk pregnancies, who we'd met when we'd had Victoria, was not working there anymore. She had decided to move on to a new academic role at a medical school. I took the news as a blow; I had liked her. We would meet the new doctor who specialised in high-risk pregnancies, who had recently started working there. I hoped she would be good because the idea of seeing midwives again distressed me already. However, I was more relaxed about meeting the old doctors I was familiar with.

Before I got pregnant, I assumed I was ready to go back to it all. When the time arrived to go back to the maternity department, I could not deal with the mental pressure. I found the two hours average waiting time in that stuffy waiting area a bit of a killer. I had never received any valuable information from them; in my particular case, it was such a waste of time. Before I got pregnant, I presumed I was psychologically ready to go through all it all again, hospital-wise. I was not.

My head was already spinning with all my previous experiences with the midwives: the four times I had been tested to check my blood type; all the blood tests to prove I didn't have HIV when they could not give me any information about checking for toxoplasmosis or group B streptococcus, when both can kill the baby; the unsupervised trainee midwife who contaminated all the blood samples; the one who insisted that Victoria's head was her bottom and she was not breech, when we had around seven scans to prove the opposite; the one who wanted to turn the baby when this was not recommended by the Royal College of Obstetricians; the delay of my C-section by seven hours because a particular group of midwives did not talk to another group. Then there was the time when they couldn't find a Thames midwife for the C-section although the doctor, anaesthetist, and pregnant couple were waiting in the theatre; the wrong information about my C-section: stitches, procedure, and recovery; the one who took the drip from my hand to check my blood pressure, causing a fountain of blood that covered everything;

the ones who had squeezed my breast painfully to try to get milk out when there was no milk, and not knowing why I was not able to breastfeed. All my questions to them were always answered with either, 'I don't know, I'll find out and tell you next time' or 'you should talk to a doctor about that'. I positively did not need any more of it. The recall of all the previous failures was with me day and night, playing in my mind like a never-ending movie. I wanted it to stop but I was powerless against it.

When we went to St Thomas' for the NHS scan at week twelve, there was a new blood test to check for genetic abnormalities. The technician was convinced the baby was far too big, so it could not be only twelve weeks old. We explained why we were confident it was; we were 100 per cent sure of the conception date and we had been seeing Dr Hamilton for weeks. We told the technician she should contact Dr Hamilton, since they were both at the same hospital, if she needed proper medical details. A copy of all the previous scans and our appointments with her were in my hospital file.

She went away 'to talk to *other people*' within her department, she explained. When she came back, she backdated our conception date to two weeks before what we had told her.

We insisted that was not possible. I had asked Dr Hamilton if I could have had a fertile day on the monitor on 3 April, if I had been pregnant three weeks earlier. She claimed that was impossible. We did try to explain this again.

We were patronised and told the doctors knew better than us. We left it there. We were happy, anyway, to be two weeks ahead according to them, which meant we could try to schedule the C-section two weeks before the due date rather than when they prefer to do it on the NHS. Two weeks less of pregnancy, two weeks nearer to success.

Usually, when the twelve-week scan is done, there is a monitor in which the woman can look at the baby. That day, the monitor wasn't working in the room where we were, and I didn't get to see the baby. Michael did; he went around to look into the technician's screen. Michael said the baby was moving a lot; in fact, it was moving so much the technician could not get proper measurements. We were asked to go for a walk and come back again after one hour; fingers crossed the baby would be a bit sleepy and she could measure it correctly. When we came back, the blood test results were ready. All came back clear: no Down's Syndrome or Trisomy 13, Trisomy 18, or any other health issues.

We were assured it was now just about impossible for anything to go wrong. All was developing appropriately with the baby: heart, lungs, brain, limbs. This was a successful pregnancy with a healthy baby. We were safe. The baby was safe.

I cannot find words to describe our happiness. We walked along the Thames on our way to a celebratory dinner. While we walked, we phoned our parents, brothers, the rest of the family, and friends. It had been forever since we had called the family to give them good news. Countless calls to give the bad news, such as: 'By the way, I never told you I was pregnant once again – things did not work for us, as usual. I had another operation.' Everybody was thrilled for us.

We agreed not to tell Victoria. She was too young, far too impatient for several months of waiting. Victoria was three years old at the time, and she was definitely good at eavesdropping. She heard us talking to our neighbours; she was captivated with the idea of having a little sister – she decided it was a girl. Victoria did not talk to us about it to start with, it was all in her drawings; now it was Mummy, Daddy, Victoria, and little sister. She could not wait to meet the new baby.

The end of the happy affair

My first meeting with the obstetrician team at St Thomas' went well. I met two trainee doctors, who were doing the appointments together. They were well informed; they knew about my history and operations, including my cartilage removal. All the information was in my folder, they told me. That was what I had always been told previously, and that my hospital number was the same, when having either NHS appointments or private appointments. Consequently, all the information was there, clearly available to any member of staff.

My second meeting at hospital with the new specialist

doctor in high-risk pregnancies was a downright different affair. I was about eighteen to nineteen weeks pregnant – according to their records; seventeen to eighteen according to our own dates.

Our meeting started awkwardly when she told me I was not a high-risk pregnancy – apparently to reassure me. She claimed she had no knowledge of any of my privately done operations because this was the NHS. I told her I had the same hospital number, folder, and online files for both NHS and private visits; also, I had been told as much by doctors on both sides previously, including at my appointment two weeks earlier within her department.

Confident that we were going to have our second baby and that I was enjoying my final pregnancy, we were organising ourselves, and on account of our track record of getting pregnant with ease but miscarrying even more easily, we had decided we should go for sterilisation after having this baby. There were some leaflets at the hospital suggesting that if a woman wanted to be sterilised, it was a good opportunity to do it during a C-section. Other doctors had mentioned this possibility after my last miscarriage. This suited me well. When reading about female and male sterilisation, it seemed there was less chance of secondary complications for women than men.

I asked for a C-section to be added to my birth plan and whether I could have a sterilisation procedure at the same time, obviously oblivious to what was going to come in the next few days. I explained the reasons: I had read that it was an option, and it would be one less operation for me. Two children were enough for us because of my miscarriage problems, my age, and how easily I got pregnant. I explained that Michael and I had discussed it and agreed it was the right option for us. I was being organised. Planning. That is what calms me down. Talking about it made me feel closer to a successful pregnancy. I could plan for the next stage in my life. All was going to end well this time. Due to my medical history with pregnancies, I was certain a C-section was the safest option for my baby.

Since 2011, the NICE guidelines for NHS hospitals state that women have the right to choose a C-section on the grounds of anxiety or other personal or medical factors. In 2019, many hospitals still do not follow these guidelines. It has been widely reported that, ultimately, the paid-offs costs millions to the NHS and their total value of the settlements is much higher than doing the investment and the right procedures in the first place. The Sunday Times reported in 2022 that the UK has the highest infant mortality rate in Europe since 2015, *'perhaps due to our natural commitment to natural birth'.*

The doctor's reply to me was, 'I do not think you want to be pregnant. I think you do not love your child.' I have never felt so insulted and treated unfairly in all my life.

I could not possibly write in detail about the meeting. I find it genuinely upsetting even now. I wrote a letter of complaint at the time that I never sent. Michael told me it was better to forget about the whole episode and move on since it was not going to change the outcome. I did not agree with that. I asked him many times to read the letter and correct any mistakes in it. I did not want to send a letter that was badly written; I was being patronised enough the way it was. I should have found somebody else to check it for me, but I was concerned and embarrassed to give my letter to a person who may find the subject difficult or too personal.

I regret very much not having sent the letter. It was the lowest of times and finding the strength to be proactive was far too hard. I was encouraged by other doctors to write an official letter of complaint weeks later. I should have done it, if not for me, for other women in the same situation; for my beloved child who did not make it.

I have added my letter at the end of this chapter, which I do not think I am going to read again, never mind any grammar mistakes. Maybe one day I'll be able to talk about the whole incident, but that day is not now. Nor tomorrow.

During the meeting, the doctor did not check the foetal heartbeat or suggest a scan or do any other physical examination on me – such as touching my belly or monitoring my blood pressure and my heart rate. I knew a foetal heartbeat check-up was part of all medical appointments at that stage of a pregnancy. I did not mention anything at the time about it, though, because as far as this doctor was concerned, our conversation was already going thoroughly wrong. I did not dare to ask and start a new argument. I had a monitor at home, the same one I used for Victoria's pregnancy. Therefore, I could check myself at home, as I had already done a few times.

This doctor was asked – once it was known the baby was dead seven days after my appointment with her – why she had not checked the foetal heartbeat since it was a standard practice. Her explanation was that she preferred not to do it because sometimes it is difficult to find the heartbeat and she did not want to make women nervous.

She was also asked why she had told me I was not a high-risk pregnancy case, when it was obvious that this was the case: that was why I was assigned to the high-risk pregnancy department and I was having an appointment with a high-risk pregnancy obstetrician. Rather than reassuring me, she had at the very least confused me. If you know you are a high-risk pregnancy, every test counts, and if a doctor struggles to hear the foetal heartbeat, she should keep on trying or arrange an ultrasound scan immediately if she suspects a pregnancy failure. Regrettably, if you cannot find a heartbeat, in some cases, that may be because there *is* no heartbeat. It is part of the job of a high-risk pregnancy doctor to have to communicate professionally with nervous women.

I decided during my appointment with her that I was not going back to St Thomas'. If that was the expert doctor who was going to help me, I had no help. I feared for my baby's life. This person was not somebody whose eyes and ears were open enough to spot early problems and save the life of my baby.

The next day, I called a couple of private hospitals in London and asked for information regarding their maternity packages to be sent to me. We were going to a friend's wedding in the Lake District that week and left London for a long weekend. I would decide which hospital to go to when we came back.

I was unable to sleep. I lay awake during the night, stroking my belly, my eyes wide open I was so scared. I kept telling myself I needed to calm down for the sake of the baby, but I could not. I was angry. I was desperate. My meeting with the doctor was distressing, her comments and her attitude were unexpected and shocking; I had gone to hospital to place the safety of my unborn child in the hands of a doctor, to trust the wellbeing of my most precious treasure to her expertise, and I left hospital in despair and feeling very alone and angry after being told I did not love my baby.

For the next nights, I did not sleep more than a few minutes at a time. I had a dream one of those nights. There was a bird cage; its door was open. A little colourful bird was flying outside the cage. I moved nearer to the cage. I could see other beautiful birds inside. I love little birds; I had them as a child and let them fly around my room. I looked inside and counted six birds. But something was wrong, it did not look good; five of them were losing their colours, they were turning grey, they did not move, their eyes were closed. One was still beautiful and colourful. It looked at me, perched on the door frame, considering whether to come out of the cage. I asked it to come out, to fly away with the other bird before it too goes grey. It was hesitant, not sure whether to come out. I could see its colour fading away. *Please come out before you turn grey,* I thought.

Three days later, on the day we were travelling up north, a brown spot appeared. It looked dry, a dark brown. I hoped it was a bit of wax left over from my waxing the day before, and part of me was not concerned about it; the other part did not even dare to consider anything else.

The following day, it happened twice. I was sure it could not be wax. We came back to London after the wedding on a Saturday evening. I found it more difficult to find the baby's heartbeat. It was still early days, and I appreciated it was not always easy: the baby was still small and, depending on its position, it was sometimes trickier to find the heartbeat. The morning afterwards, another brown dry patch came out. I checked my pregnancy books, which read that bleeding or discharge in the second term of pregnancy was riskier than in the first term. I could not hear a heartbeat using the heartbeat monitor on the Sunday morning.

I phoned the hospital and left a message for the Thames midwives. I did not know where else to go; on top of everything, it was a Sunday. There was a number at the front of the maternity book; it was meant to be a twenty-four-seven contact with your specialist midwife. We searched online for a private clinic in which to have an ultrasound scan while we waited for a call back. Although we found some clinics open for other health-related matters, no one could do a scan on a Sunday.

In the end, I phoned the Early Pregnancy Unit at St Thomas', since the Thames midwives still hadn't called me back after leaving a second message. I knew they were not able to do scans on a Sunday at the time. The nurse at the Early Pregnancy Unit confirmed over the telephone their policy of no ultrasound scans on Sundays – there were no technicians or doctors there. I was told to pop in and they could check the heartbeat for me.

It was better than nothing; I could not find it myself and the nurses there were more experienced than me, so surely knew how to do it better. We were going to Cornwall the next day to take Victoria for her first beach holiday. It was still the same country if there were problems with the pregnancy; however, we didn't know the area at all and we didn't want to be hunting for a hospital while we were there.

I went to St Thomas' on my own, as Michael and Victoria went to run errands. When I arrived, it was quiet. I didn't see anybody else waiting.

A nurse came into the room. She tried to listen to the heartbeat. She could not find it. She looked unsure but told me everything would be fine: 'It may have been the monitor not working properly.' She started touching my belly, and her expression appeared to be even more apprehensive. I had likewise noticed that my belly was looking saggy rather than the full, hard, and stretched, more typical pregnancy belly.

She explained that she was going to talk to another nurse to see if she could have better luck finding the heartbeat. She came back after several minutes. The nurse was busy with another pregnant woman. We were going to wait for her. I was left there on my own, lying on a bed. I knew but I did not want to know.

When the door opened next, the nurse was accompanied by a trainee doctor, who told me he would do an ultrasound scan. It may sound dramatic, but I knew then it was over – for a scan to take place, against all the rules and regulations, there on a Sunday. We moved to a different room for the scan. There was no screen for me to look at. Both of them looked at their screen and said nothing for a few minutes. It was only silence. The doctor kept moving the transducer around my body.

I spoke, in the end, tired of the deadly silence: 'The baby is gone.' I could not bring myself to pronounce the word 'dead'.

He replied, 'No, it is there.'

'Yes, but if it is there and it is dead, it is gone *forever*.'

He did not reply. He did not want to announce the news. Or maybe he was not allowed to. Instead, he stood up and said, 'I am going to leave now; the nurse will talk to you.'

The nurse told me my baby was dead.

I was told – days later – that the trainee doctor got told off for doing the scan, as did the nurse who had asked him to do it. I defended them both vigorously. They were only trying to help; it was their duty as health workers, even if there was red tape or paperwork to fill in, or health and safety regulations. I asked if there was any doubt that the baby could have been alive, meaning the trainee doctor and nurse had got it wrong. 'No, not a chance,' I was assured, 'they were correct.' No, there was no doubt about it.

'Could they have somehow damaged my pregnancy with their actions if the baby had been alive?' I asked.

'No, that was not possible,' came the reply.

'Please can somebody explain to me what they did wrong?' I insisted. 'I am wholly grateful to both for doing their jobs.'

As things stand, I am still waiting for the Thames midwives to call back.

I sent a text message to Michael. *The baby is gone.* I did not want to talk. He said he would come to pick me up. I preferred to walk to meet him and Victoria. I came out of the hospital through the main entrance and sat on a bench facing the river. That beautiful view, again, of the Thames and Big Ben, some tall trees around me, tourists passing by with their cameras. I was a spectator of life. Life must go on. Life was moving along in front of my eyes, but I could not move anymore. I was heartbroken.

After a few minutes, I wondered what to do next, who to talk to. I needed a friendly face. I did not want to be there. I contemplated whether to call Dr Hamilton to organise an

ERPC. It was Sunday; I was not sure it was right to contact her. Sure, it was not right to contact her; sure, I did not know what else to do. I tried my luck and sent her a text message. Dr Hamilton replied straight away. She was shocked – that made two of us.

A few days later, I had the ERPC done. I needed to have an official second ultrasound scan to confirm the baby was dead. No lucky surprises there. Dr Hamilton told me she had been considering a post-mortem examination of the foetus but decided against it because the results were going to show that most of the organs were immature, which at that stage was to be expected in any case. She explained that doctors need a foetus of at least twenty-two weeks to get any proper data regarding possible malfunctioning issues with the internal organs.

A few days later, we met Dr Hamilton again for a follow-up on the operation results and the standard DNA analysis of the foetus to look for genetic issues. It was the three of us, Michael, me, and Victoria, since we could not find anyone to take care of her. In a way, Victoria made the meeting less difficult, since, rather than sitting down to have a continuous tough conversation, every two seconds I had to take some medical tool from her that she had grabbed. She was pretty good at interrupting conversations and asking her own questions.

As Dr Hamilton had predicted, nothing new was found on the foetus. She could not tell me when the baby had died.

When a foetus dies, it starts shrinking rapidly, meaning it was unclear from its size whether it had died right after our week twelve scan or more recently. Likewise, it was unclear whether its current size was because of the length of time it had been dead or whether it had not been growing because something was not working properly. She could not tell me either whether the baby was alive when I'd had my ill-fated meeting with the obstetrician. Because of this, our questions regarding when or why the baby had died were unanswered. That is why the lack of monitoring when I'd met the obstetrician was even more crucial.

I had been picking up the baby's heartbeat until the Sunday I went to the Early Pregnancy Unit. I was not finding it easy to locate, especially on the days after my final pregnancy meeting, and the heart rate was very variable too – which did not happen with Victoria. It was suggested to me that it might not have been a heartbeat but something else that I was picking up with my heartbeat monitor. True, I am not an expert – but it could not have been my own heartbeat, which I picked up also at half the speed. A foetus' heartbeat is rapid; Victoria's was always over 150 beats per minute (bpm). I have a good heartbeat of around 60 bpm, and it reaches over 140 bpm when I run for over twenty-five minutes on the running machine, by which time I am out of breath and red as a tomato. My heartbeat goes down fast when I stop running; within under a minute I am under 100 bpm.

I dared to ask, 'Was it a boy?' Dr Hamilton replied that

was the case. Two healthy boys lost. She didn't think the lack of drugs was an issue, since, in any case, the baby had died at a time when I would no longer have been on the drugs.

I had stopped acupuncture around week twelve as I didn't feel a connection with my new acupuncturist. I regret that; I could at least have looked for somebody else. However, my body felt positively strong after week twelve, and I was ultra-confident. I believed I could do it by myself once I was over the usual notorious early twelve weeks.

I had many questions. Since nobody could prove the opposite, I was – I still am – convinced that it was the aftermath of the disastrous meeting with the obstetrician that ended my pregnancy. All was fine before – or if it was not, we will never know because that doctor never checked when she had the opportunity to do so. I blame her – at least in part – and that meeting. A foetal heart rate check at that time could have exonerated her from my accusations, if I had been told, for instance, 'the baby was dead before you came to see me' or 'the baby's heart was not working properly, therefore he was never going to make it'.

Dr Hamilton suggested we should consider adoption. Another solution was to try IVF – privately, because of my age and the fact that we had a child already. That way, the egg and sperm could be screened for any genetic problems, as in my fourth and fifth pregnancies we had had two different genetic issues, so the screening would be justified. A female foetus could be chosen, in my case medically allowed, since we had lost two healthy boys for no clear reason.

The old issues were back in my mind. I have tirelessly tortured myself for letting the first foetus go without doing any tests. I wish I had known of a place where it could have been taken for analysis, since, in view of my later miscarriages, any information could have given us more clues about what was going on. In times of distress, it is easy to make the wrong decision, but putting it in the freezer or fridge while finding a test lab could have perhaps given us some answers. For example, out of the four miscarriages we had any knowledge about, I had lost two healthy boys; it was suggested, as some doctors believe (though some others altogether dismiss), that some women miscarry only boys. Was the first one a boy or a girl? Was it genetically okay? Since we'd had two foetuses with different chromosome problems – one with Down's Syndrome, another chromosome 13 – this was not enough to reach any conclusion. However, another foetus, with or without genetic problems, could have maybe answered a few questions.

As a multiple miscarriage sufferer, I do believe more should be done to find out why they happen. The books state that half of miscarriages occur because of a problem with the foetus, but what about the other half? Would you cross a road if you have a 50 per cent chance of being run over?

New research published in 2020 by Warwick Medical School on a new treatment for multiple miscarriage using a new class of diabetic drugs with a successful pilot clinical trial was described in a national newspaper as the first successful development in the last 40 years.

Michael and I had said IVF was not for us from day one of our journey. I had read about how stressful it was. The success rate was not that encouraging either. We were emotionally drained, and the thought of having a stillbirth was paralysing. It remained unclear whether the problem lay with the foetuses or my body. If it was my body, what were the guarantees that implanting a robust female embryo was going to survive within me?

We told Dr Hamilton we had had enough; we were going to concentrate on Victoria. We had to leave it there. That was it. No more. Finito.

Letter of complaint

To whom it may concern,

I am writing this letter to you after much consideration, not because I do not feel the utmost conviction about my complaint but mainly because I would like to forget the ordeal I have been through in the last four years as a result of my six miscarriages and the poor care I received from Dr C. in my last pregnancy. Had my pregnancy not failed, I would have changed maternity hospitals after my appointment with her.

This is a short background of my pregnancy problems: I have an amazing daughter, although the pregnancy was a complicated one, and I have suffered six miscarriages, two before my daughter and four after. After years of meeting doctors, privately and on the NHS, it seems unclear why this is happening to me and my husband.

I met Dr C. on 20 June. I was keen to discuss a Caesarean for medical reasons: I have had five miscarriages, four ERPCs, a uterine operation to remove a septum, and a Caesarean for my daughter at St Thomas' under the care of Dr Susan Bewley. During my daughter's pregnancy an early miscarriage started, which was confirmed by a scan, and I suffered some bleeding when I was eight months pregnant. All the doctors that I had until then met in Spain and England, both privately and on the NHS, recommended a Caesarean and considered any future pregnancy high-risk.

Dr C. got agitated when I mentioned my uterine operation, which was performed privately by Dr Judith Hamilton at Nuffield House. She seemed angry and mentioned that this was the NHS and she did not have any information about it. I told her, as I have been told before and after meeting her by staff members at Nuffield House, that all the information should be in my records. I have doubled-checked again if this information is correct and I have been assured it is. That I opted to do my uterine operation and two ERPCs privately did save me a lot of waiting time, in the case of the ERPC, an average of two weeks, and also saved the NHS money, which is much needed in the current economic crisis.

When I told her I believed the safest option for my baby was to be delivered by Caesarean, Dr C.'s reaction was out of order. She said that my pregnancy was not high-risk and that there were NHS regulations; if I wanted a Caesarean, I should go private. When I insisted that my pregnancy was high-risk, she said that was not up to her, but the decision would go to the head of the midwives. I do not understand how this can be the case, since a midwife is not an obstetrician and, in any case, a midwife would never perform the operation. I have spoken with a GP and a high-ranking doctor, and they both disagree with Dr C.

However, the main impetus for my complaint is that Dr C. subsequently suggested to me that I did not love my child and I did not want to be pregnant. That is the most outrageous suggestion I have heard in my entire life. It is out of order to say something like that to a pregnant woman who, in my case, has gone through four years of stress, disappointment, and mourning for, at the time, five miscarriages. In any case, this is the twenty-first century, and if a woman doesn't want to be pregnant, she is not pregnant. Dr C.'s next comment expressed an intention to send me to see a psychiatrist, which is not only bizarre but entirely out of order. If her justification for the NHS wanting to save money is to call pregnant women insane, I sadly conclude that the standard of care at St Thomas' has fallen to very low levels.

I had another question on the day, which was whether it was clinically possible for me to be sterilised at the same time as having a CS, as I had read on some leaflets, and that if this was the case, I would like to consider the option. This has been a decision that my husband and I have thought about carefully. I was extremely surprised by Dr C.'s reaction. She said she did not recommend that I do this since my baby could die soon after being born or I may decide in the future to get a new husband and have children with him. I do not think these were appropriate comments, and although I stated that to her, she kept mentioning them. I am a happily married woman who will be thirty-nine years old at the end of the year, and if I were ever going to get a new husband, I would be more likely to exchange photographs of our grandchildren with him than to have my own children with him. I found her comments patronising and insulting.

Dr C. did not check the heartbeat of my baby or perform a scan on me. This is the only time that I had an appointment with an obstetrician in which this was not done. I had the most terrible week after my appointment, not being able to have a moment of tranquillity as I remembered my appointment. I was unable to sleep, my levels of stress were high, and I was nervously checking other hospitals and care options for my pregnancy, since I was determined I was never going to meet her again. On Thursday 24 June, I noticed a small discharge, and after three days of it and not getting any response to my messages to the Thames midwives, I went to the Early Pregnancy Unit, where I was told that my baby had died. The date of death is not exactly known, although doctors said it is possible it had died it before I had my meeting with Dr C. If she had been doing her duty as a doctor rather than patronising me, denying that I had a high-risk pregnancy and calling me insane, she could have found out the sad news for me. That is an obstetrician's role, and although I understand that nothing could have been done to save my baby, I expect an obstetrician to check.

The only offer from Dr C. was to organise a blood test to know my blood type, which I found irritating and pointless since it has been recorded several times and does not change. She said it was NHS regulations – this was her most repeated comment that afternoon – and she personally had no opinion on it. Why a test to confirm something we already knew but no scan or heartbeat check?

In summary, I met an obstetrician who delegated a decision about a CS to a midwife, who was not interested in checking how my pregnancy was doing, who decided at the beginning of our meeting that I needed psychological help, and who seemed annoyed about my private operations. What about applying her obstetrician knowledge to my case? Or even her common sense?

I have no interest in hearing from Dr C., and I will undoubtedly not use St Thomas' as a maternity unit as long as she is there. I had two reasons to write this letter: the first one is to leave no doubt that I DID love my child; in fact, I still love him even though he is gone forever. Second, maybe my letter can save another pregnant woman who is searching for good and professional obstetric care, from going through the same horrible appointment that I had to go through.

CLOSURE

If I had done anything different, would it have changed the final outcome? The million-dollar question. Could I have done something to make me feel better? Lots. I regret not speaking up. Should I have done something better? Probably, but I knew no better.

What did I learn through this journey? I realised I am not good at stopping to think. I was not able to calm down. I was (rightly so) frustrated. The cocktail of not complaining, keeping it all inside, together with the sadness of each miscarriage, was lethal.

There are obvious actions I might have taken – obvious in retrospect: for example, not checking whether I was pregnant the first time. I had all the signs, but I did not find the time to buy a pregnancy test – yet how long does it take to buy a pregnancy test? How long does it take to tick on a spa form that I might be pregnant? The fast pace of modern life does not always pay off.

Then again, I remember Dr Hamilton telling me that, in her vast experience of taking care of pregnant women, she has seen everything: for some women, with the most difficult pregnancies that nobody expects are going to succeed, their pregnancy goes ahead. For others, in spite of how hard the couple try and how much they follow the medical advice, things still do not work out.

In my last pregnancy, all seemed to be going perfectly well. However, emotionally, I was a wreck. With no clear reason for my miscarriages, after my long journey, I found myself in the 50 per cent of women who suffer from idiopathic miscarriage (their miscarriages remain unexplained despite all the investigations). *Early Pregnancy Issues* by Geeta Kumar and Bidyut Kumar suggests emotional support supplemented by ultrasound scans for those women, which, according to their book, gives success rates of 70 to 80 per cent. This is the same advice suggested by *The New England Journal of Medicine* in their recurrent miscarriage study. I did not have any support like that. I felt so alone. I did not speak up about going private – at that point, it was *what the doctor ordered*. Could a better set-up on my last pregnancy have given us a better outcome? We will never know. It makes me sad to consider it.

I stopped acupuncture because I could not find a replacement for Kylie. I wanted to run away from everything, and I did not feel a connection with anybody new. I was exhausted. However, acupuncture is the only thing I can think of that separated my successful pregnancy from the others.

Should I have waited for longer before getting pregnant again, to give my body a rest? I had no issues about my age, although I kept on being told that age was an issue – for all women, not only in my case – although all fertility tests I went through were more than encouraging. Every young doctor I met along the way told me this was happening to me as a consequence of my age. The senior doctors denied that was the case; I was told that when a woman is over forty-three years old, other age issues start affecting a pregnancy, but not at my age. A while ago, I read about Professor Evelyn Telfer's work at Edinburgh University, where new evidence suggests that women's ovaries may be able to grow new eggs. Other scientists dispute these findings; however, can you imagine if we old cows are old cows no more?

I could not have had babies any earlier with Michael since I only met my husband a little more than a year before I first fell pregnant. Fate protected me so I didn't have any children with any of my ex-partners. I do not even want to imagine that scenario.

I was thankful we had agreed we would never do IVF before we started. At least we had a clear line we did not want to cross. If the decision had not been in black and white in my mind, I might have jumped into an extra onerous journey.

I never got pregnant again. I did hope, for a long time, for another unplanned lucky pregnancy. It is known that when you gave up on something, that is when it happens. But it never did. I guess it was my body telling me it had had enough. If I had been rich, I would have rented a surrogate bump, if my eggs could have been used. That idea is too freaky for my husband. I don't care; I would have put the embryo in a bird's nest if that was going to keep it safe.

A friend of mine is currently pregnant. For the first time in years, my reaction when I found out was one of real happiness for her. No more feeling sorry for myself. She is in her early forties, and she is not having it easy. There are bleeding issues, and she has run to A&E and the Early Pregnancy Unit a few times. She has had several ultrasound scans. She has been told the problem is a cervical ectropion and that the pregnancy is safe. Every time she tells me about her problems, I cannot control my stress. I get panic attacks and remember my own experiences. If I feel like that with somebody else's baby, no prizes for guessing that I could not cope with a difficult new pregnancy of my own, emotionally or physically.

When Treacle died, Victoria was not concerned to start with. 'Treacle died, but that's not a problem. Daddy's going to take her to hospital, and she's going to be fine,' she told everybody. I had the same blind faith in doctors and hospitals to start with.

If I have learnt anything from my experience, it is that doctors are not always right. Some of them are superb; others do not have a clue or even bother to read your file before giving you advice. We learnt the hard way during the last four miscarriages and when we dealt with my mother-in-law's illness. Within weeks of her passing away, my father-in-law's Alzheimer's disease took over. Doctors, hospitals, care homes, social services, and councils. It was relentless. Dealing with care homes is depressing to the point that we both decided, if the time comes, we'd rather go on a short trip to Switzerland.

In the future, if I get to talk to any professional, I will not take his or her opinion for granted. It is worth asking for a second opinion. How to treat a health problem varies in different countries and hospitals. New advancements happen continually, and some hospitals are quicker than others to adopt new advice and new technologies.

I remember flying to Spain while having a miscarriage, after I was told to go home and continue with my life as normal. That was out of order. I would accept a 'sorry we don't have a budget to help you here, but the next hospital up the road can help you'. If you cannot offer me ERPC/SMM due to budget restrictions, let me know about other hospitals with a different policy, but do not send me home to take it easy and 'enjoy' life as normal. I would never get upset if a doctor tells me he does not know the answer to something or that, due to budget restrictions, I need to go to a different place. I appreciate honesty. In times of illness and when you feel you have no knowledge of the subject, it is easy to believe what somebody, with a high opinion of themselves, lectures at you.

I learnt it is worth doing research myself. Having some knowledge will help you ask the right questions. While doctors should always be far ahead than you and their knowledge should be better than yours, unfortunately, that is not always the case, and it pays to do your homework.

My biggest regret is how much I kept to myself. This is the advice I would give to a younger me: if you do not agree with a doctor, ask for a second opinion. Check hospitals, check maternity success rates, read reports, ask for feedback, make up your own mind. Remind people (when required) that you do not need to be patronised, that you have a brain. It will make you happier to be in control of the situation, and any complaint that you make may also help the next pregnant woman who comes along. It is your life: fight for it, make it better, love yourself. Take notes; write down names, dates, contrasting opinions – says the assertive, grumpy old woman.

In my humble opinion, the most negative aspect of motherhood has nothing to do with children or post-pregnancy bellies. It is the brutal way job opportunities dry up as soon as the baby arrives.

I was – I will always be – angry at the unfairness once I became a mother. I have not long ago admitted to myself that I would not have stopped working if I had known the outcome; I was now out of the race. Forever. On the other hand, I am not sure how realistic this view is. Without hesitation, I would have blamed my later miscarriages on me being at work.

I should have found part-time work before leaving my job. That would have given me a better chance with future employers. However, I had been looking for part-time jobs, or any jobs, for over two years by the time I left. It kills me how hard it is for women. Not only for women; the main issue is that children need proper care and suffer more than any adult from the lack of it. They are the real losers here, becoming a burden that needs to be shifted around so that companies don't need to be flexible. In Norway today, the father of a child is entitled to three months' paternity leave, which cannot be passed on to the mother. What a brilliant idea. As I write in

February 2020, the Finnish government is trying to change the maternity allowance in Finland and make it compulsory to be share fifty per cent between each member of the couple to avoid work discrimination of young females. How brilliant if all men, potentially, could take several paternity leaves during their whole working life.

Childcare and jobs have a complicated relationship as well, since nurseries and schools will call you immediately if your child is feeling unwell. You have to run to school, where he or she will be sitting in the reception area, waiting for you. In our school, there is a 48-hour, do-not-bring-your-child-back policy if the child is sick or has a fever or diarrhoea, even if the child is happily jumping up and down at home. Children learn very quickly what to say, such as a friend of my daughter who lied to their teacher, saying she had fallen over in the playground and had hit her head, which was hurting a lot. Banging your head gets you out of school. Very handy for children to know about.

My daughter would be ill and at home for around eighteen days each term until she had her tonsils and adenoids removed. That is over fifty days a year. What employer would cope with something like that?

The last two of our au pairs had to be sent home; in fact, once smartphones became affordable, that was the end of good au pairs or us. The girls were constantly hidden in their room on their phone, messaging their friends abroad rather than trying to make new friends in London, leaving them teary and isolated. Victoria was told on several occasions, 'I cannot play with you, I am busy on my phone'. One of them got lost in London for over an hour with our daughter, while the other one nearly left Victoria twice on the train platform. Contrary to our first au pairs, the new ones didn't know how to cook, even very simple dishes, and they did not know how to do any house chores. One of them kept putting the rubbish and recycling bits in the wrong bins because she would put the bags in the bins while watching videos on her phone. They were children themselves who needed to be taken care of.

A good nanny makes more money than my best full-time salary, so it wasn't an option for us. At one time, I had a part-time exam invigilator job, but lack of childcare meant I even had to stop doing that. I despaired that I was not even able to hold on to a job that only took up ten weeks a year.

When the time comes, I will tell my daughter about women's issues and about the types of job available, as well as the advantages and disadvantages of being self-employed. The old adage is true: *get your house and finances in order before you get into the job of having children*. A while ago, there was an outcry when the headmistress of a top independent schools for girls said it is not true that women can have it all and we need to teach the girls the price of motherhood. She was right: it is better to talk to the girls honestly about this from day one to help them be organised and to have a clear picture of the situation.

When I started university, I was only seventeen years

old. My new best friend told me she was 'going to marry and have two children' – I remember she had even decided on her husband's career. I told her I was never going to get married or have children. In the end, she never got the husband or the children.

When I was young, I would have liked some advice on careers, starting a company, being a freelancer, and so forth, but of course I would in all likelihood not have listened that much or followed any advice about managing children and a career or about going for jobs that were better for women with children, since, in my mind, I never ever was going to get married or have children. I think I was too naïve, thinking that, for women, discrimination was something from the Victorian times.

Likewise, women should absolutely talk more about miscarriage – but what about men? If there is not much help available for women, there is none for men: man up, forget it, they are told. A male friend told me what a hard time he was going through; his daughter-in-law had had a miscarriage. The most important thing for her was that nobody else knew about it; it was a dark secret. He was asked to make a wooden coffin so that the foetus could be buried in the garden. He worked on it with a broken heart. He told me he needed to talk to somebody about what had happened, even if he was not allowed to. It was a relief for him to share it, and he chose me because he knew my history.

As I said that my husband did not want to participate in

this book. I told him it would be great if he could write a few pages about his experience to add his male point of view. He refused, and he does not like the fact that I am doing it myself. He told me that if it helps with my healing, that is fine – as long as I do not publish under my real name. But I am not doing it for healing. Actually, it is not helping with any manner of healing. The fact that I write about it for hours, followed by endless rewriting and proofreading, in a daily effort to remember all the details, means I am a like mouse running on a wheel and I have to go through all of it again. I am writing the book because I am the voice of my dead children, who, like all the other miscarried babies, deserve some more medical investigation to avoid women going through these very traumatic experiences in silence and with no clinical explanation that could at least help with the healing and give some understanding of why it happened. I would like to think that my babies didn't die in vain and that somebody cared about them.

Completely changing the subject and the gloomy mood, after a lifetime's wait, I finally got my dog. Good things come to those who wait, and Freya has not disappointed. She is an absolute beauty, always happy to see me, always cheerful.

I tried for Freya to have puppies, as I could see myself helping with the birth and having a dozen puppies running around the house, plus perhaps starting a new business from home. Of course, with my history, it didn't work; she refused to get pregnant and has zero interest in boy dogs. She is clever. She is a career dog. I might get a second dog, so she has some furry company – once my husband gets used to the idea of having more animals in the house than people.

I am committed to making my life better. Contentment is my key word; it worked for the golden generation. I have taken mindfulness courses. I do my best to practise daily. While it is not a magic quick fix, it still works wonders. Reluctantly, I practise yoga. It has never been my first choice, although I admit it does good.

I realise time is the only healer; time helps me to see these experiences as a deeply sad part of my life rather than a burning constant pain that controls my life. It has taken me years, but I can look at babies now and enjoy their cuteness. Only weeks after one of my own miscarriages, one of my brothers sent me a message to say his partner was pregnant with their second baby. I was at a restaurant and started crying (that will teach me to look at my phone on nights out). When he told me recently that baby number three is on her way, I was elated with happiness, and I cannot wait to meet her.

I wish to finish this book soon and put my memories to rest. I am planning a cheerful project next; I am going to have another go at finding a job, the best of the rest: private Spanish tutor, dog walker, afterschool stand-in grandma. Or maybe I will write a cheery romcom?

ADOPTION

After the fifth miscarriage, Michael and I had already spoken about adopting. It had proven too difficult for us to have a baby of our own, but there were children out there in need of love. Could we be a match for one of them?

A few days after my fifth miscarriage, I phoned a reputable adoption agency and left a message. I received a call back within hours. Our conversation went differently to what I had expected, given that their website was so positive about adoption, full of photographs of overjoyed parents and their adopted children, as well as encouraging videos of laughing families. The lady on the phone was negative – or assertive. She disclosed that, as an agency, they did not have any children themselves. Their job was to place the children that councils could not place. Therefore, only the most difficult children were available. We would have a choice of older children with either mental problems or disabilities, or whose parents were drug addicts, alcoholics, or had several mental problems themselves, including schizophrenia; children who had grown up with domestic violence in the family; or children whose parents had severe learning difficulties. I was told by the caller that, having a child of her own, she would never adopt because it causes endless problems.

There was also a rule that, after a highly distressing experience, such as the death of a close relative, severe illness, separation, or divorce, the prospective parents would need a transitional period of two years before they were allowed to start the adoption process. Since the miscarriages were recent, we did not fit the right profile. I was upset about this conversation. It could surely not be completely hopeless for these children? We decided at the time not to take it any further, since, in any case, we were not allowed to.

After my sixth and final miscarriage, Dr Hamilton asked whether we had thought of adoption. It was still at the back of our minds, but now I was unsure after the conversation when contacting the adoption agency. On that occasion, it was too early to take such an important decision. Months later, I saw an advert in a newspaper for an adoption and fostering open day jointly run by three London councils. I decided to go along. I was excited about it. The law had changed not long before to make the adoption process faster. Potentially, the whole process, including the adoption itself, could take place in less than a year. In some cases, it could be a sorter process than planning a pregnancy and coming back home with your baby from hospital.

It was a mixed day. Again, I was more confused when I left than when I arrived. It was a morning event, with several speakers and time to ask questions. The session was well attended, both by prospective parents and social services staff. Some of the council workers were positive; they made me think adoption could be a rewarding process for everybody involved. However, the last speaker was the Head of Adoption Services. She was dreadfully negative, making comments such as, 'the adoption target of the government is too tight; it's unfair on social services'; 'there are not enough young children to be adopted'; 'forget about getting a baby or young child'; 'you can only adopt a child of the same race as the parents – you are mainly white here, and all our children are mix-race or non-white'. She even stated, 'All the children are mentally damaged. Your life will be miserable.'

Either the prospective mother or father had to be a full-time, stay-at-home parent. You cannot adopt if you work, even if your job is part-time. Having help at home, such as an au pair or nanny or any other paid help, is not well thought of. It means you are not that interested in the child or have other priorities. Once again, following the outpouring of negative information, I lay the idea of adoption to rest.

Back home, I spoke to one of my neighbours. They have three children of their own and adopted a black child back in the 1990s. The children are now all adults in their forties. Their story is worth repeating if only for the madness of it. One of their sons had a best friend at school when he was around nine years old, a little boy called Matt. Matt's mum suddenly died, and his father, who was married to his mum and living with them, said he didn't want to take care of him. My neighbours offered to take Matt into their home. The council didn't agree with this because Matt was black and my neighbours are white. 'He should be with a black family,' they were told.

Matt had other relatives in the UK besides his father; however, none of them were available or willing to take care of him. The council placed him with two different black foster families. Both families rejected him after a few months. They complained that he was misbehaving. On each occasion, Matt came back to live with my neighbours. Matt never gave them any problems. He was a perfectly settled and well-behaved child. He made it clear that he wanted to live with them. My neighbours asked to adopt him. The father did not oppose this. Once again, the council said no because he was black and the family was white.

In the end, the boy was sent to Uganda to live with a distant uncle. In a hut with no water or electricity. My neighbours paid for him to go to school over there; they supported him in every possible way for years. When Matt was eighteen years old, he took a plane back to Heathrow. When he landed, he telephoned them: 'I am back, I am eighteen; please can you adopt me now? And by the way, can you come and pick me up from the airport?' A happy ending for a bizarre story.

I used to look at an adoption website every day; sometimes, if I woke up in the middle of the night, I used to go to the computer and spend a long time looking at the little faces. On the one hand, it felt wrong that the children were listed on a page – like choosing a dog or a cat to buy online; on the other hand, it was heart-breaking to see the little children's pictures. They all looked cute and charming. I had my favourite children that I would adopt if I could. When they disappeared from the website, I told myself I was pleased for them. They had a new, good family. Some children stayed on the website for months.

A few months later, I contacted the same adoption agency I had first spoken to after my fifth miscarriage. They were doing an open day where I could have a one-to-one chat with a member of their team. I got to talk to a positive, cheerful lady. I explained to her my previous experiences, including the telephone call with her agency. She told me she was not surprised I had been put off adopting with that sort of comment.

We had two main options, I was advised; if we wanted a baby, girls were in higher demand than boys, and it would be quicker to go for a boy. We could try for *concurrent planning*, meaning we could have a baby placed with us as 'foster parents' while the court decided what was in the best interest of the baby: either to return to his or her parents or stay with the foster parents, who could proceed to adopt the baby once a decision had been taken by the judge. The downside was that the court might decide it was safe for the baby to be returned to its birth parents. During this process, the baby would have to be taken for regular visits with their birth parents by the foster parents. These meetings could be up to three times a week. This is not an easy situation for anyone.

Bruised by my previous intense experiences, I could not face twelve months on the edge, wondering whether this baby in our care had to be given back. It felt in a way similar to a miscarriage – you might lose the baby that you love, but in this case, the baby is a living person you have taken care of for months, who potentially is going back to a family where she or he might not be as well treated and loved as in your own family. The odds were that the baby would stay with the foster parents, but nothing would be in black and white for months.

The lady answered lots of my questions; in particular, we were concerned about the process of being approved for adoption. We had read that ex-partners had to be contacted; they would be asked to give a reference. We did not consider that was fair on us. We believed it was no business of our ex-boyfriends or ex-girlfriends to know about our struggle to have a family – they were *ex* for a reason. After further questioning regarding our referees, I was told we needed four people each to give a character reference. That did not include ex-partners unless there was a child in common with them. This sounded fairer.

The other option was choosing an older child; again, a boy would be quicker, I was reminded. I was open to boys or girls. I came back home and spoke to Michael. We decided to give it a go. The next step was to start the ball rolling, meaning that somebody would come to our house and interview both of us together and look at our home to see whether it was suitable. You cannot adopt unless you have a spare room that can become the child's bedroom. No sharing with siblings allowed. If you do not have a spare room but are considering moving to a new house, we were informed you have to move first and then apply for adoption. I was thrilled. It was an exciting moment for me.

We learnt that the council keeps a file on every adopted child, and when they are about twelve years old, they receive a letter explaining about their adoption and their birth parents' background. I thought this would be unsettling for a child at such a complicated adolescent age. The council believes it is important to create this constant reminder for the child that they are adopted. I do not think it matters or agree with it. You are a child with a family that loves you.

I contacted an old friend in Spain; I used to babysit his older adopted son before moving to London. Years later, they adopted a baby girl too. I wanted to know his opinion about the whole process and whether they or their children had to be in contact with the birth parents. That was not the case in Spain. There are no letters. My friends had no knowledge of the background of their children, as stipulated by law. It is completely the opposite there.

Their adopted boy had ADHD (attention-deficit hyperactivity disorder). He was about six years old when he started having problems at school. He struggled throughout his childhood and teenage years. He did not do well at school. At that time, no one knew enough about ADHD to know how to deal with it. He is a wonderful boy, though, caring and sociable. School was just not his thing. The baby girl was fine;

she grew up to be a perfectly balanced teenager who had never given them a problem – his words.

I also spoke to an American friend of mine. She was adopted as a baby and has an older adopted brother. She said she was more than happy with her adopted family. She added that she has no interest in knowing who her mother was or meeting her; she is grateful she was not aborted by her birth mother, but that's all. Michael has some adopted cousins, too; their adopted parents are *their parents*; that is how they see it.

I had a lengthy conversation with a cousin of mine, who is a psychologist. She does lots of work with teenagers and the children of drug addicts and alcoholic parents. She revealed that some of them are great children, ashamed of their parents' behaviour and doing their best in life. Others are 'beyond help', as she put it. She confessed that she could see through them. She'd know if they would likely end up like their parents or in jail in a few years' time. There is nothing anybody can do to help them, as much as social services, schools, and psychologists try.

She was, nevertheless, positive about adoption: 'It is like having your own child. You can have a healthy child or you can have a sickly child who came from your own genes.' We should be prepared for everything and accept it all with good grace.

The formal interview with the agency did not go as well as I expected. It was a case of Dr Jekyll and Mr Hyde every time I spoke to an adoption service worker. I could never guess who

I was going to speak to. This new lady was extremely negative about us adopting, because we had our own child already, and then told us again how all children who needed to be adopted were seriously damaged. She gave us a list to choose from: were we prepared to choose a child from an alcoholic family, a drug-addict family, from a family with several mental problems or learning difficulties? She could not have been more negative about everything.

Once we were approved – which would take two to six months, depending on how quickly all paperwork and assessments got done – we would have access to a database, she explained, where we could see all the children available for adoption in the country. There, we could pick out a child we thought we liked and who would be a good match for our family. The catch was that, at the same time, there could be many other couples choosing the same child; in which case, a bidding process would start – with all families explaining why they were the best option for the child.

It was wrong. It was like when I use eBay to bid for an item, but in this case, it was a real child. I could not bear the idea.

When she left, I was very angry. They put the fear in you. Maybe it is done to get rid of people who, they assume, will not be able to cope with the whole process – but for me, it was the wrong approach. Michael said, 'we could beat the system'; for sure, we would be the best choice for a child if we chose one. I did not agree with his view. We had been told that having an au pair was not well received by councils; the fact that we had a child was going against us too; and we might be too posh for their liking. I couldn't see myself bidding for children. I went a bit over the top and tore all the adoption papers into pieces. That was it.

It was not right for us, or it was not the right time. For the time being, we have forgotten about adoption. However, I have not ruled out the idea of becoming a foster parent at some point in the future.

Children need love, so what does it matter if they do not look like you or if they are a different colour? If a child by the age of two has not established a loving connection with somebody, it will be difficult for them to do so later in life. When I see those terrible images of orphanages, it breaks my heart. Why do you even have to adopt a little baby? A three-year-old is also in need of love, and he or she may have eighty years in front of them to give that love back to you.

BEING A MUM

Why add a chapter on being a mother – you might exclaim or even complain – in a book about miscarriage? I have debated with myself long and hard about it. This whole appendix has been in, out, and back in again. At some point, it was part of the chronological flow of the story as it happened. However, in the end, I decided against mixing the joy and tribulations of being a parent with my story of miscarriages, although having a child profoundly changes the nature of trying for another pregnancy. For example, my own health was poor for over four years. Victoria was constantly ill, and I managed to catch every single one of her colds. That put an extra strain on my tired body when it came to trying for another baby.

I also didn't want to discuss the joys and pains of taking care of an infant when the reader may be mourning a lost baby.

However, in the end, it is part of my story and the madness of pregnancies and becoming a mother. With these thoughts in mind, I separated this discussion from the main body of the book and have kept only the sections I would have liked to know about before becoming a mother. If this content is not for you, you can safely ignore it. If you decide to read it, it may give you a laugh or give you some insights into what may be coming to you in a not-too-distant future.

I guess if I'd had easy-going pregnancies, I would

have been reading happy books about babies and toddlers. However, my aim was different when I was pregnant with Victoria. Get the baby out and alive and the rest will be a piece of cake.

The aftermath of pregnancy — first early days

Sudden death scare

I was not concerned about Sudden Infant Death Syndrome (SIDS) before being a mum. I was aware of it, of course, but I appreciated it was rare.

While I was pregnant with Victoria, I was bombarded with information about it in hospital and in parenting magazines, to the point where I was sick with nerves, thinking that I might get my baby only for her to die in her sleep. I realised it was unusual. It happens more when the mother smokes and when she is young; for once, being young was not an advantage. I learnt it that happens more in boys than girls. It is also more common in babies of a small size, which was not going to be the case with my girl.

Still, I spent the first few months waking up in the middle of the night, fearful of SIDS, getting up to go to my daughter's nursery to touch her belly. I considered buying an electrical gadget, advertised in parenting magazines, to be placed between the mattress and the sheet that would beep as soon as the baby stopped breathing. I did not purchase it because Dr Peppas told me that sometimes babies stop breathing for a few seconds, which is okay, it is the way a baby's heart works at that early stage. We may have experienced false alarms, which I realised would do no good to the health of my own heart.

During the pregnancy, we were endlessly told that babies must sleep on their back to protect them from sudden death. Victoria started rolling on her side by herself when she was less than two months old. By three months, she could roll over, and I often found her sleeping on her front. One night, I took her to my bed and put her on top of my own belly to keep her from turning over. I was lying in bed, awake all night, listening to her breathing.

In the seventies, in Spain, the advice was the opposite: my brothers and I were put to sleep on our bellies, in case the baby vomits in its sleep, and the three of us are still standing. When one of my mother's elderly uncles came to see my new-born brother, he said, 'It's a girl.' 'No, it's a boy,' my mother replied. 'It has to be a girl to be sleeping face down,' the uncle said. 'If you put a boy to sleep like that, his willy will get flat.' I guess in the 1940s they had other concerns. My brother has managed to produce two daughters, so I imagine the sleeping position was safe for him in all respects.

Moses, cots, and the family bed

One of my sweetest memories: what a marvellous feeling, having my tiny baby sleeping next to me. She would glue her whole body to mine, from head, arms, belly, and knees to her toes. If I moved away one centimetre to have some breathing space, five seconds later, she would move to be next to me.

She also slept much longer if she was in bed with us. She would sleep for five hours without waking up. She was 3kg 560g when she was born; we fed her on formula milk and our nights were better than we had anticipated.

I believe she liked our bed's thick mattress too. The Moses basket would not be comfortable for her for a long time – a small, plastic-covered mattress on top of a thin wooden frame. She didn't like to be put in it. She was restless and woke up often. In the end, she was either in a proper cot, with a thick mattress and a larger frame, or with us in our bed.

We had read hundreds of times in books and been told by family, friends, and midwives that we should never let her sleep in our bed. Some argued we would never get her out of our bed, yet she didn't hang around much. When she was a little over two months, she decided she wanted more space; rather than sticking herself to me, she would move away a bit to get some room for herself. Soon she was sleeping in her own cot in her nursery.

As she got older, she would still come to our room in the middle of the night if she wanted a cuddle. She always went back to her room afterwards because she preferred being in her own room with all her toys and blankets.

Hormones

My hormones were barmy for three months after the pregnancy. Picky, over-alert, volatile, nervous, insecure. However, I didn't notice that was the case at the time. If somebody had asked me how I was (did anybody ask me how I was? I don't remember anybody asking me how I was feeling), I would have replied, 'Fine, normal as always, getting on with my life.' It was only much later, when the madness was over – and there was no more vaginal bleeding – I had the capacity to understand what was going on with me. At the time, I didn't have a clue it was happening. It must have been great to be around me.

My life was exhausting. I wanted some time for myself. I would have liked to blow-dry my hair in the mornings or to have gone for a quiet walk by myself. But there was not time for any of that, and no doubt I was overtired.

Post-pregnancy body

The craziest article I read after giving birth was about a new trend: having an operation to make your belly button smaller again. The article claimed it could never be the cute little thing it was before a pregnancy without it. It was hilarious. I couldn't spend my life worrying about the size of my belly button. Isn't it enough to worry about the size of my derriere? And my boobs? And my belly? Absolutely no time left to worry about a belly button.

First Christmas dinner as a mum

I was constantly trying to be Little Miss House Perfect after I had Victoria. I love Christmas, and I remember dearly Christmas evenings at my great aunt and great uncle's house as a child with all my beloved elderly relatives – I never appreciated the time it takes to make Christmas dinner for seventeen people. I wanted to replicate the same magic in my own house.

I was in the kitchen with my seven-week-old baby and using my foot to rock an unsettled Victoria in her baby rocker on the kitchen floor next to me, while whisking a cake with one hand, reading the recipe for it in a cookery magazine, and holding the telephone between my shoulder and ear to talk to Michael, who was at work on Christmas Eve. He wanted to know what time to pick up his parents the next day. I was in a state of panic, then suddenly Christmas lunch had to be cancelled because my mother-in-law was feeling dreadful; she ended up spending a few days in hospital during the Christmas period, and my sister-in-law, who was due to give birth soon, said she was not feeling up to joining us.

I was relieved that I could stop whisking when I found out nobody was going to make it to our house. Officially, I was disappointed. In reality, I welcomed the unexpectedly simple Christmas.

Now you can relax while we all go to the football or on shopping trip

My mother had come to help for six weeks. I must confess, I wasn't sure about it when she suggested it. My brother and his wife had insisted how much I was going to need her, but the idea sounded excessive. We didn't believe we were going to need any help – us, being clever people. How much help do you need to take care of a little baby that sleeps most of the time anyway?

They were right. I could not have done it without her help. Even just to be able to say, 'I'm going to the supermarket to buy some food, can you stay with the baby?' Or getting my mother to take care of the baby while I had a shower. When she left in December to go back to Spain and her own job, I felt like a hopeless baby myself. In retrospect, I could have done with a few more weeks of her help.

In the early days, when Victoria was three months old, I was going to be the do-it-all perfect mother. I refused to have any childcare, since babies sleep a lot anyway and play by themselves. I was deluded.

Soon, I was going insane, exhausted, and nutty; I did not have a single minute for myself or my personal development to-do list. My other brother, his girlfriend, and a cousin came over to see the baby after Christmas. There I was, trying not to look too edgy, cooking breakfast, lunch, and dinner for everybody, and hoping for some childcare relief – I did not get a single minute.

One Saturday morning, after I made breakfast for all of us and had a messy kitchen to tidy up, two of our visitors took off to Oxford Street to go shopping, while the other one and Michael went off to a football match. Before they left, they told me, 'Now that we're all off, you can relax.' I badly wanted to cry. Everybody was off to have fun; I was stuck in the house with the baby, the messy kitchen, and the burden of cooking dinner for everybody.

Rock the baby in the car seat if she goes to sleep like that

Most of my stress and doubts about what to do and what not to do as a new mum were the result of other people's advice. Everybody had an opinion – a strong opinion – and I was left confused. I was bored of reading how you should never – ever – take babies for a drive in the car or put them in the car seat to make them sleep.

Victoria slept blissfully for the first four months – it being a cold winter, she was mainly at home; we didn't go to any baby groups. Afterwards, when we started being more sociable and meeting other babies, Victoria seemed to have a permanent cough that kept waking her up at night. We started a lengthy bad period of colds that went on to last for five years.

One night, desperate and tired after trying everything to get her to sleep, we said, 'Okay, enough is enough, let's go for a night ride.' We placed the car seat in her cot, ready to put her in. As soon as we sat Victoria in it, she stopped crying and fell asleep. Magic. We wondered, 'Oh no, what do we do now? Do we move her? Go for the drive?' We left her in the car seat in her cot, sleeping blissfully.

That was the beginning of three or four months of the car seat, a Maxi Cosy, being placed in her room if she couldn't sleep. We used it for rocking her; many nights, we left her sleeping in it with classical music playing on the radio. It worked well, but I was concerned – okay, more like frenziedly anxious – driving my husband insane about whether we should stop doing it because everybody insisted it was a terrible mistake and we would have to do it for the rest of our lives.

Overnight, when Victoria was nine months old, she refused to sit in the car seat at bedtime. She slept contentedly all by herself in her bed.

Whatever works for you, do it. Those well-intentioned people giving advice are not there with you when you have not slept in days. Every baby is different, every family is different; we all have our own personal circumstances.

Children grow in intervals

I was surprised to hear about the way babies grow – in spurts rather than steadily day after day. Influenced by my mother's obsession with being fat, I used to write down every single time Victoria had milk or food and the amount.

I wanted to keep track of her eating and know her timetable so that we could organise ourselves properly – when to be ready, when it was okay to go out, and so forth.

Out of the blue, Victoria would ask for double the milk or food for a couple of weeks, and afterwards, she would go back to normal. She always grew taller afterwards. It amazed me that her body realised when she needed to eat more. Luckily for babies, they do not have to read magazines about beach ready bodies. They can just enjoy their food.

Victoria had been a good eater from the first day. She was healthy and had no serious illnesses until she was about eight months old, when she got tonsillitis. Then, she had a constant cough and couldn't eat more than a few spoons of food each day. For about two weeks, she ate almost nothing and lost a lot of weight. It was a deeply worrying time. A boy I used to babysit in Spain once ended up in hospital on a drip because of not eating after getting an illness. I did not want to end up there. Once Victoria got better, she started to eat again; she recovered her weight smoothly. She still does the same. I keep calm now. Not wanting to eat is a sign that she is unwell – even if she does not look unwell yet.

Baby clothes

Zero-to-three-month-old baby clothes are tiny. Victoria didn't fit into them, not even as a new-born. Babies grow amazingly quickly. It was surprising to see that, from one week to the next, all her clothes were on the small side. Parents get plenty of presents before babies are born. My sister-in-law received twenty-one little dresses that her daughter never wore because she was already too big for them when she was born. It is not worth buying too many small-sized clothes. It is better to get clothes of different sizes.

Sell the clothes

I didn't attend any NCT (National Childbirth Trust) groups – not my thing. However, I used their 'nearly new' market to sell plenty of baby stuff, from clothes to prams to toys, as well as maternity clothes. I set up my stand on a Saturday morning for a fee of around £30 to sell clothes and small items. They sold my big items – cots, prams, chairs – for me (keeping 30 per cent). The market got fairly busy, and I sold tons of things – some of them for not much, considering how much they had cost, but overall it was a good return.

Deciding to sell the baby stuff was not a big deal. Of course, I have kept dresses and toys that have a special meaning for me. I kept items that I hoped I could reuse for a second baby for quite a long time. The idea of selling them came from the need to make some space by de-cluttering the house.

Virus incubation

It was a tough learning curve to find out that illnesses can take up to two weeks to incubate. When Victoria suddenly became tired and refused to keep walking down the street or she behaved erratically or grumpy, it was better to take it easy and understand that maybe there was a reason for it, rather than telling her off.

The first ever puree

Exciting time for a mum: the first ever puree – baby rice puree. Once again, I had been reading books about it to be well informed. The expert advice said: *do not try to give them their first puree when they are hungry, because they will get frustrated and angry. Instead, give it to them when they are not hungry*. 'Okay, I'll do that,' I thought, 'Though it feels a bit odd because Victoria is not going to want to eat it when she isn't hungry.' Nevertheless, there I stood with my video camera ready and her first puree in the bowl when it was not her usual time to eat. It was a disaster. She was not hungry; clearly, she was not interested. I ended up with a video of her looking angry, screaming her head off and refusing to eat the baby puree. I deleted the recording.

After the disaster, I decided to change strategy and follow my instinct. 'Tomorrow, I am going to do my own thing; I am going to give the puree to her when she is hungry, instead of the milk,' I decided. It was easy. She loved it, and as a result that video is cheerful.

Write things down to make memories

Get yourself a nice notebook in which to write down all those funny things that your child does or says. It will be a treasure to keep for life; your child might enjoy reading it as an adult too. I have a list of the first twenty-seven words that Victoria learnt. I love reading it.

Music lessons at three months

There was something that we all had in common at my local Monkey Music class for three-to nine-month-old babies. It was not that we all had a baby and wanted them to become the next Mozart. No, it was that we were all first-time mothers wasting our money.

I wish I could have taken photographs. It was hilarious. A very enthusiastic lady sang to an audience of twelve babies, staring at the ceiling, sleeping, crying, or sucking their toes. Not a single one paid a second of attention to what was going on during the whole half hour. They were all given different instruments or toys for each song. They invariably put these in their mouths to suck on, helping to spread their viruses to one to another. That was when Victoria's illnesses started.

Sure, babies benefit from music, but I should have kept it simple by singing the nursery songs myself at home. Cheaper and more hygienic. Nothing against Monkey Music – Victoria went there for about three years, and as an older child, she enjoyed it hugely.

Let the husband change the nappy – even if it takes him fifteen minutes

I remember the first time I babysat in my early twenties. I was taking care of a six-month-old baby. The time arrived when I needed to change his nappy. No problem, I said. I did a great job, I believed. Until I lifted the baby and the nappy dropped to the floor. Not a problem – 'I just needed to put it on a little bit tighter.' I started fastening it again tighter on the left side, and, oh! – the strap didn't reach the right side. I struggled for a few minutes with the puzzling nappy. Luckily, I only had a baby as a witness, who kindly kept our secret.

Years later, when my husband had a go at changing our tiny baby's nappy and it took him at least fifteen minutes (yes, I was timing him on my watch because I was going insane), I let him do it, hoping that next time it might only take him fourteen minutes. I had learnt an important lesson from my brother and sister-in-law. Since she was better at it than he was, she always told him, 'I'll do it, I'm much faster.' Over time, she got even faster, and my brother was even happier not to do it. After having two children, he never had to change a single nappy. He says with a cheeky grin, 'I wasn't fast enough.'

Yummy daddies

If half of the stay-at-home parents were dads, it would be seen as a much more respectable job. I know a yummy dad – a stay-at-home dad. He claimed he had more patience and was calmer than his wife. His wife was also keener on her job than he was on his. Thus, he quit to become the stay-at-home parent. He was happy. His children were happy too.

A colleague at work used to repeat the same story during our chats. He wanted to be a stay-at-home dad. He and his wife agreed that the one who was making less money once they had a baby was going to be the lucky winner. He won the money race in the end, though, and his wife stayed at home. When he offered to swap places for the second baby, she politely refused.

The toddler years

First visit to the GP

Our GP practice had been a disappointment for a long time. They didn't answer the phone, and it was nearly impossible to get an appointment; when you did get to see a doctor, they were not helpful. The care I received for my miscarriages was poor. Michael's experience had been disappointing too, as had that of all our neighbours – it gave us something to talk about during neighbourhood parties.

When Victoria was two weeks old, I noticed she had some tiny red spots on the right-hand side of her chest. I called the surgery first thing on a Monday morning, but I couldn't get an appointment until Friday. I explained it was for a new-born baby. Still, without asking me what the problem was, I was told there were no appointments available. I went there on Friday. By then, Victoria's whole body was covered in these spots, and she was looking poorly. I was told when I arrived that my appointment was only going to be with a nurse – who couldn't give any medication. I made a big fuss; a GP appointment became instantaneously available.

Unfortunately, it was with my old friend, the shoulder-shrugging doctor of my second miscarriage. He told me the spots were not important, they would go by themselves in time. It was the same 'I don't have a clue, I don't give a sh*t' attitude he had had with me. I left the surgery upset; I decided not to go back home but to walk to a newly opened surgery half an hour away. I registered Victoria and we saw a GP on the same day. The GP was horrified when he saw her skin. He couldn't understand why the other doctor hadn't done anything about it. 'The spots were never going to go by themselves,' he exclaimed, although it was nothing too dangerous – new-born skin is very delicate, and she needed treatment for a couple of weeks.

I was not the only one having trouble with a GP. A friend's baby daughter was constantly vomiting and having diarrhoea. She took her several times to the doctor, to be told it was normal for babies to be sick. In the end, she was told by her GP that there was nothing wrong with the baby; she was the problem, she had post-natal depression, and she needed antidepressants. She left the surgery and decided to go private. She discovered her baby was, and will be for life, severely allergic to a number of foods, including milk and wheat.

I mention her experience – I could add many others – because I found the way that some doctors talked to us, first-time mothers, to be completely patronising. Oh, you inexperienced mum – you panic too much, you know nothing!

GP diagnosis

Victoria started nursery when she was nearly three years old. After about one week there, I noticed she had five large, dark red spots, three under her arm and two on her chest. We had moved GP surgeries again since a new one had opened about two minutes' walk from our house, but it proved impossible to get an appointment.

I contacted the out-of-hours doctor the next day, on a Saturday morning. The doctor said over the telephone, 'It's probably chicken pox, although what you're describing doesn't sound like chicken pox spots, but what else is it going to be? She needs to be out of nursery for a week.'

On Sunday, we decided to take her to a walk-in clinic. The doctor was annoyed and told us that, since my daughter had already been diagnosed with chicken pox, there was no need for us to come there. I said, 'The diagnosis was made over the phone, and somebody should have a look in person, since it could be something else.' He looked, then reported, 'It's probably chicken pox, as the other doctor said over the phone, although,' he added, 'those five spots do not look like chicken pox spots to me.'

Victoria missed a week of school for starters, plus, a second week at home, since new spots kept appearing. However, they didn't burst or become itchy. Otherwise, she did not look bad at all. Victoria was active and chirpy, she had no fever, or any other symptoms, and she was eating nicely.

The two of us were about to travel. We were going to be whisked off to an Italian villa for Victoria to do clothes modelling for a toddler's clothes shop. I had spotted an advert in a shop window asking for models; we went for a casting and smiley Victoria was chosen.

I went to the local GP surgery to explain the situation. The new doctor we saw responded, 'Oh yes! Two doctors have already said it's chicken pox, so it must be chicken pox, although those spots do not look like chicken pox spots.'

I replied, 'It has been more than two weeks now.'

He said, 'Victoria is not allowed to travel because everybody on the plane would get chicken pox.' He insisted on giving me a letter to say she was not allowed to travel on the grounds of illness. We lost the contract, and the clothes company didn't phone again.

Two days later, we found out the reason for the mysterious chicken pox. Michael was at work when he saw a flea going down his shirtsleeve. He had been complaining about some mysterious itchy spots on his feet. He thought he had foot fungus, and he was using some cream for it. What did they both have? Flea bites from Treacle, who was angry at having a child in the house and used to rub herself on my daughter's bed when we were not around. A full disinfection of the house put an end to both the mysterious 'chicken pox' and the foot fungus.

Adenoids and tonsils

Since she was a few months old, we had terrible winters, with Victoria coughing for hours at night. It would start in October and finish in May. For about three years, when she started nursery and then school, she missed an average of eighteen days per term because she was constantly coughing. She could literally cough for two hours non-stop. I took her to the GP several times only to be told that it was a virus: 'Nothing can be done – it's normal, children get sick a lot.' Each time I was told she could have an over-the-counter cough syrup but nothing else. She had tonsillitis about four or five times as a consequence of the continuous illness and lack of medicine. It repeatedly ended with her taking antibiotics.

We were desperate – not only frightened for her but also tired from the sleepless nights, added to my being pregnant three more times. I was also continuously unwell with the same cough; my body was weak after the pregnancies and operations. I wanted to talk to a specialist, not to a general practitioner.

When we went on holiday to Spain in the summer, I

went to see a paediatrician. He charged €50. We arrived at our appointment, and after he'd completed the mandatory form with the usual measurements and information, he announced, 'I know why you are here.' I was sceptical: how could he be so sure why we were there just by looking at us? 'She has adenoids,' he explained. 'Can you see how she breathes and the shape of her nose? I'm sure that when I check her throat, I'll see large tonsils too. I think I am going to be right.' He was.

His advice was to wait for a few more months, for Victoria to be five years old, because when some children grow, they get the extra space they need in their nose and throat to breathe better. However, he continued, 'In your daughter's case, in my opinion, she will need both to be removed because they are far too large.'

I could not believe that no one else had spotted this in three years, when he had spotted it just by looking at her. He gave me some proper cough medicine, which was practically miraculous and stopped 80 per cent of her coughing. I bought supplies for years every time we went to Spain on a holiday.

When talking about it with our GP on a later visit, the excuse she gave for not knowing that Victoria had adenoids was that the surgery did not have the 'equipment' to check. The equipment is a pen-sized stick with a light at one end. If they didn't have the equipment, why did they not refer us to somebody else with the equipment? As for tonsils, no specialist equipment is needed to see them, apart from two working eyes and a bit of willing.

We waited until Victoria was a bit older and then went to see an ENT (ears, nose, and throat) specialist, or otolaryngologist, in London. He had the same reaction when he saw Victoria as the paediatrician had had in Spain: 'I can see she has adenoids just by looking at the shape of her nose.' When Victoria had an operation to remove both her adenoids and tonsils, the surgeon told us she had the largest set he had ever seen.

After the operation, she needed two weeks off school, and her breathing improved so dramatically that she didn't look like the same person when she was sleeping. She hasn't missed school because of a cold for years now.

Two friends of mine went through a difficult time as well, with over a year of constant visits to the GP to be told that their children only had a cough. A cough that lasted for hours each night and brought endless sleepless weeks. Both children ended up in A&E many times and eventually in hospital for over a week. It was not just a cough, it was asthma.

One of the mothers needed to take a week off work to be with her son when he was in intensive care in hospital. She was told by her company, for whom she had worked full-time for eleven years, without ever taking any days off sick, that the next time she had to take time off because of her son, it would have to count as annual holiday. Would it have been the same if she had been in intensive care herself?

On the other side of the coin, another friend's child was told she had asthma and put on medication; however, her illness has nothing to do with asthma and the medication she was given made things worse. She ended up in hospital with pneumonia for two weeks, on a drip, and in an oxygen mask.

The medical journal *The Lancet* published an article in 2013 in which they placed the UK at bottom of a list of fifteen European Union countries for an excessive number of children's deaths, blaming this on the lack of paediatric training for GPs or on GPs not working closely with child specialists.

Eventually, I sent a letter of complaint to our current local GP surgery, with a summary of our three years with them. I also added that our two local pharmacists had also complained about the poor service they provided and how difficult it was to contact them when there were issues with prescriptions. I asked the surgery for a reply in writing, addressing my concerns. I received a telephone call: they did not want to reply in writing, they thought it was better for all of us to meet and have a chat. Before we could set up that meeting, the surgery closed down, and it has remained unoccupied for years.

Snakes on a plane

We took Victoria on a plane for the first time when she was four months old, on a trip to Spain to meet her relatives. My grandmother was over the moon. After a few days,

Michael flew back to London, but Victoria and I stayed on a little longer.

On the day we were due to fly back, we had a bumpy, two-hour car journey to reach the airport. I was feeling unwell and assumed it was the car journey. Victoria and I checked in and passed through customs. It was a small airport, so there were no shops in the departure area. I was a first-time mother on a first-time trip abroad. Did I think of packing extra clothes for Victoria? No. Did I pack extra milk? No. Did I think of bringing any medicines in my handbag in case she was not feeling well? No.

I only had the little bottle of milk that I was allowed to take with me through customs, which I gave to her just before getting on the plane. Fingers crossed she would sleep all the way back to London. She gulped the entire bottle and then vomited all over her clothes. I cleaned her up the best I could. We got on the plane, and I sat down with Victoria on my lap. She looked to the right, then to the left, and started screaming her head off for the thirty minutes that it took the plane to take off. Once in the air, she continued screaming for the duration of the flight, just short of two hours, except for twenty minutes when she fell asleep exhausted. It was horrific.

I was feeling terrible myself. At the time, I figured it was a combination of the car trip and the embarrassment on the plane – people were looking at me and making comments. The woman sitting next to us put her headphones on. My head was spinning. My ears were blocked; sometimes I could see Victoria was crying loudly, but I couldn't hear her.

Michael picked us up at the airport. We were stuck in traffic for the next three hours, during which Victoria was either screaming or sleeping. We stopped to buy some Calpol; Michael had brought some milk in the car. This helped calm Victoria a bit. The next day, we both woke up with a fever of over 39°C. In Spain, we had visited an old relative who had been very ill with flu the week before we'd met. We were poorly for several days, which explained the behaviour on the plane and our ill health.

Now Victoria is brilliant on planes. But not before having a nightmare year when she decided she didn't want to put on her seat belt for take-off or landing, when she would scream and kick her legs for minutes.

Oh joy! – when other children have a tantrum in public

I had always been one of those people who could not stand a screaming child next to me, before having a child myself. I bought my first iPod after a Christmas flight that was full of overexcited children who were running up and down the aisle. When I got my own screaming child, I found it mortifying. There was no way to escape it. Soon, I did not mind other children having a tantrum. In fact, I was overjoyed, thinking, 'Thank goodness it's not my child screaming today.'

Brilliant! It's not maternal instinct – it's pure relief when it's somebody else's problem.

I came across an article by Dr Harvey Karp, a renowned American paediatrician, who suggested throwing tantrums when your children do, which I had already been doing. I made faces, waved my arms, lay on the floor, and lifted my legs. Of course, I only did all of this if there were no other adults nearby. Victoria found it amusing, and sometimes embarrassing. It always worked.

Your life will be a constant birthday party

In the old days, when I was a child, when it was the birthday of another girl in my class, I was invited to her party if I was her friend. I was not developmentally damaged when I wasn't invited to the party of somebody who was not my friend in the first place.

These days, says the old girl, birthday parties are like a mini wedding, where everybody in the class gets invited to avoid traumatising any of the children. You may be asked to pay £400 to £600 to host a two-hour party. Not for everybody's pocket – and a rip-off.

In my daughter's school, we get a list at the beginning of the year with everyone's addresses and birthdays, which works well for arranging joint parties. The positive side of these parties is getting to know the other parents; we've started some long-term friendships at them.

Sugar rush at birthday parties

I, the chocoholic, managed not to give my daughter any chocolate or sweets – other than raisins – until she was three years old.

Once Victoria started school it became impossible to stick to a good diet. The reasons for celebrations are endless – international cultural days, to each girl's birthday, to the last day of term, somebody leaving the school, egg hunting, cooking at school, celebrations, prizes, charity events, school fairs. It never ends.

The first time I experienced first-hand the so-called sugar rush was alarming. We were at one of our first birthday party invites. At the beginning of the party, all the children behaved well; they had fun with an entertainer. After a meal of high-calorific carbohydrate foods, a large number of sugary drinks and sweets, nobody could be blamed for thinking they could not possibly be the same children. The screaming, the running, the arguments, the crying.

Although it is difficult, it is better to avoid sugar as much as possible, in particular in the evening, if you want your child to go to sleep. I should apply the same principle to myself.

F*ck it mummy

There we were, two young ladies driving in a car to go to a ballet class for three-year-olds. Yes, I did it not once but twice, *mea culpa*. Twice, a car driving too fast and carelessly almost crashed into us; twice I said, 'F*ck it!'

Afterwards, Victoria knew *just* when to say 'it'. Such as when nearly falling over because of an uneven pavement, or opening the fridge and finding that there's no juice left … Although I never laughed, got angry, or told her not to use that phrase, it took several weeks for her to stop repeating it.

I find driving in London stressful. I do long drives on the school run, and there is not a week when we don't see an accident or dangerous driving. Last term, my car was hit twice; they were very apologetic. Luckily, I was in the car by myself at the time. Victoria now calls it 'explicit driving with Mummy'. Oops.

Your mother does not always know better

We left Victoria with my mother and my aunt to go to a music concert. I told them Victoria had her dinner at six p.m. and her bath at half past six. She needed to be in bed by seven p.m. It was a Friday when she was always overtired and grumpy after a whole week in nursery. She was three years old; her bedtime was already a late one by English standards.

When I told them the schedule, my mother told me she knew better! She'd had three children, she knew how to take care of them. My timetable was ridiculous. In Spain, children go to bed much later, dinner after eight p.m., bed by nine or ten p.m. The story goes that she decided to do it her way and ignore my instructions. It got to half past seven, no sight of dinner and no bath yet.

'Where is mummy?' Victoria asked.

'Mummy isn't here,' my mother replied.

That was the beginning of two hours of out-of-control screaming until an exhausted Victoria fell asleep in her clothes with no dinner and no bath. When we arrived back home, my mother and aunt were drained. Both deaf from the screaming, in a nasty mood, and blaming me for having such an unruly toddler. I asked why it was seven thirty in the evening and nothing had been done? My aunt – who has no children – told my mother quietly, 'Well, she did tell you.'

Bringing up a child to be bilingual is hard

'Children's brains are like a sponge; they absorb knowledge effortlessly,' the articles said. Well, don't get upset if it doesn't work for you. If both the mum and dad are native speakers of the same foreign language, which is spoken in the home, you might be able to bring up your children bilingual, if imperfectly so; the child's accent will not be the same as that of a native speaker and it is still a continuous struggle if the child has no intention of learning. I do not know of any child, in a mixed language marriage, that is a native speaker of both languages. Lots of arguments, classes, private teachers, and trips to see grandparents help.

For the foreign-language-speaking parent, it is not

easy either. 'You are a traitor' is something a few friends and I had been called back in Spain because our children do not speak Spanish or they are not that good at it. I have heard, from parents with older children, that it gets easier in senior school, when even if the child is not that good at the language, he or she is still better than the other children are. That is the best incentive to learn faster – to show off to their peers.

One good book

I got a few pregnancy and parenting books, read reviews of a few more, and was recommended many more. I found many of them alarming, particularly the one about not looking your baby in the eye after ten p.m. Everybody knows so much; they believe they have the right to tell you what to do, what to eat, what to think, how to feel. I am convinced there is only one type of person more patronised than a woman, and that is a pregnant woman.

I like one book about being pregnant, which is Professor Lesley Regan's book *Your Pregnancy Week by Week*, and one book about babies, *Your Baby Week by Week* by Simone Cave and Caroline Fertleman. When my baby was six weeks old, she got scared of everything. I could not put her down, not even to go to the loo. I was rather nervous about what was going on, especially after having my mother scream at me every day, 'Never hold the baby!' and 'This is your fault –

I never held or kissed you, because if you do, babies will always want to be held!'

Thanks goodness I bought that book, because it said that in week six, babies get scared and clingy because it is the first week of their lives in which they start properly looking around and seeing things. They are overwhelmed. It is a bit too much for them. Once I learnt the reason, for the rest of the week, I was captivated and felt relaxed holding my cute, little, looking-around, scared baby.

While I credit books with being useful up to a point, in particular for a first baby, personally, I learnt to take their advice with a pinch of salt. The advice changes so much: what my mother was told in the seventies is nothing like the current advice, and my daughter, if she ever becomes a mother, will certainly be told something completely different again.

Each baby is different anyway. If you have two children, what works for one may not work for the other. It is your life, your baby, your decision. If before becoming a mother you were an independent woman, with a career, knew how to pay your bills, cook your food, and enjoy your life, there is no reason why you now have to turn into a nervous idiot who needs to be told what to do all the time.

Buying my own baby scales

I did two baby weighing sessions. I was there for over an hour on each occasion, all for a thirty-second weighing and a twenty-second conversation: 'She's fine.' I did not come back. Instead, I bought a cheap pair of baby scales. As long as she was growing, all was fine.

The downside

Goodbye freedom and being the master of your destiny

After I had Victoria, I sometimes remembered my idle weekends as a single person, living in a crumbling rented studio flat near Regent's Park. On Saturday mornings, my biggest concern was whether to go the gym or lie in bed a little bit longer. Sunday morning, I had a nice croissant and an enormous newspaper to keep me busy for half the day. For the other half, I enjoyed a window-shopping trip to Selfridges or a movie at the local cinema.

I am not bitter about it – a bit nostalgic maybe. Now I have responsibilities. When I plan to do anything, my first thought is not about me but how is that going to affect my daughter? I might come across a great embroidery course – but who would take care of my daughter? My trips abroad to visit friends were out the window.

I sense my husband is making plans for the future too. We went to Paris for a break when Victoria was two years old. We left her in safe hands with my mother and the au pair. We went to Lafayette, as you do, for a quick look around. I didn't want Michael to get bored. When we left, he said to me: 'When Victoria is older, you two can go to Lafayette. I'll wait for you at a pub, having a beer.'

Sometimes, it feels like your brain has died and you've not had an interesting conversation in years

I once worked with a university professor, and every single month when he saw his pay slip in his pigeonhole, he would pick it up and wave it in the air, crying: 'This justifies everything'! I was no longer getting *everything* at the end of the month. It was all about the baby, meeting women with whom I had nothing in common and nothing to talk about apart from baby poo, baby weaning, and baby sleeping. It was hard.

I was an avid reader. Before my daughter was born, I started a newspaper subscription to avoid having to go out of the house with a baby to the newsagent if the weather wasn't good. However, I didn't open a single newspaper or book for months. Instead, I was washing, feeding, and entertaining.

Isolation

The most difficult part for me after giving birth was the isolation. I cursed not having anybody to talk with. I don't mean talking about baby nappies and baby sleeping patterns. I mean having an adult conversation or just having a laugh. The change from coming and going anywhere at five minutes notice, being a manager at work and dreaming of higher things, going to bed when I was tired and had had enough of the day, to nothing at all, for hours and hours, days, and weeks – just loneliness. Isolation. It was as if my life and previous efforts to be independent, get a good education, and a good job had disappeared into thin air. Gone with the wind.

I remember, when I was pregnant, having a conversation with a friend who had studied with me in Edinburgh. She had a two-year-old baby at the time. When I told her that I was going to use my maternity leave to read about twenty web-related books to get a new job afterwards, she looked quite surprised. She said, 'Oh, maybe you will have the time to do it. I couldn't do anything apart from taking care of my son.'

Famous last words.

Once you are a mother, you are a pest

Nearly twenty-five years ago, I stayed with a host family when I came to London to study English for a month in the summer. They had two children; the mother told me, bitterly, that she used to have a good job at a bank. She stopped working for five years to take care of her two children. Later, she was unable to find a good job. She had to work as a sales assistant in a store. It cannot be that bad, I judged.

Years later, I worked alongside an office temp. She was a fantastic worker, with amazing knowledge and skills – clearly, she was better at the job than I was, though I kept that to myself. She told me that, since having children, she had been unable to find a full-time permanent position. Nobody wanted her because she was a mother in her early forties. I came across this situation again and again. I interviewed, helped to select CVs, or took part in interview panels where I was repeatedly told by my managers 'not this one, she has children'. I am now in that situation.

'What do you do?'

This is the most dreaded question for me: 'What do you do?' I shrink when I hear it. I would rather have somebody ask me about my weight or sexual history. I can feel the heat running up my body all the way to my mouth when I reply, 'I'm a full-time mum.'

'Oh, how many children?' is usually the response.

'One.'

'Oh.'

If jobs were flexible, life would be fairer for mothers and babies

I always gave my best shot at work before and after being a mother, though there were times when I would sit and do nothing at work for various reasons, the main one being because I had nothing to do. I studied for a full-time diploma while holding one of my first administrative jobs at a university department in London, where I did half of my coursework at my work desk because I genuinely had nothing left to do; so no chance of a promotion or pay rise. It was enjoyable to be there but there were no chances of moving up.

Once, I painted the walls of my office on a Saturday afternoon when nobody else was around, tired of searching for a painter offering an affordable quote and dealing with overzealous health and safety regulations. The office was the first point of contact when somebody came to our department, but the walls were filthy. I bought a tin of white paint and did a decent job.

Other times, I did nothing purely because that was what everybody else was doing, including my manager, who liked to chit-chat. I have never understood it when companies are quoted on TV or in newspapers as saying how expensive it is for them to hire people part-time or how it is necessary for all their employees to be there all the time.

I remember when I was working and pregnant with Victoria, I tried and succeeded in completing all my annual objectives in six months. I worked relentlessly despite having a high-risk pregnancy. I liked my work. I never missed a deadline or received negative feedback. I was certain my moral responsibility was to do my best. Before I went on maternity leave, I left thousands of pounds in my budget, allocated to specific projects since I wanted to make it easier for my replacement. I then hired a competent replacement for twelve months and made him fully aware of the situation. I had a bad feeling that my budget might mysteriously disappear into the PR department once I left. I came back twelve months later to find that all the money in my budget had indeed been moved to PR before my replacement had arrived, on the day after I'd left (there were a couple of days in between me leaving and his first day at the office). Absolutely nothing had been done in twelve months. I mean, nothing – not a project, not a telephone call to check on departments, nothing at all. Not a single page of the website had been changed. I do not blame my replacement. He sussed out the situation quickly; he saw there was no money and no willingness to put any effort into the department. He had twelve fantastic months.

When I came back to work, I asked for a job share – I could work three days a week and the company could hire another manager for the other two days. My boss stated, 'That's not going to work in such a busy place; we can't afford a part-time person or to share a role.'

My two sisters-in-law managed to make their roles part-time. In Spain, by law, companies have to allow women to work part-time if they have children younger than eight years old. I thought it was going to be the same here with job sharing, but it was up to the company to decide whether that arrangement would work for them.

I was told once by a high-flyer that she never bothered to be quick or to finish things on time because it was not looked upon favourably in her company to leave work early or on time. If she had to stay late every day, what was the point in hurrying with her job?

Revisiting my old life

Becoming a mother made me revisit many experiences in my life, the whole true meaning and importance of which had escaped me before.

Women are at their most vulnerable as soon as their baby is born

I only had one bad boyfriend in my life, who told me he had hit previous girlfriends. It had been their fault, he said; they'd provoked him. He was possessive and childish. He told me I should admire him because he was a university lecturer. However, he didn't want me to study; he was keen on us getting married and having babies. I ran away for dear life. I heard he eventually got married. 'My family can get me a quiet wife,' he always bragged. He is now divorced. He doesn't have access to his children since alcohol and violence were part of his daily life. What a lucky escape I had.

Violent men may control themselves when they know you can leave them easily. As a single woman, you can leave, even if you have to sleep under a bridge. However, many violent men know that when you are at your most vulnerable, in need of help and for things to be all right for the baby, this is right time for them to strike. Violent men do not change, so run away from them.

If the man is not right, the man is not right

What a mess some women get into – and they cannot blame anybody but themselves.

I used to be friends with a fantastic woman, who was neurotically obsessed with getting a boyfriend, to the extent that men would run a mile from her after the first date. If she had only calmed down. She was such a nice, intelligent, and interesting person. She met this guy, who was ten years younger than her, unemployed, and rather nasty. My friend moved to a new house because her flatmate didn't like the way he was treating her and was being vocal about it. She bought a flat, where he stayed for free. They argued continuously, and he refused to meet any of her family or tell his family about her.

He was consistent on one thing though: from the first day until the last, he told her: 'I do not want children.' She didn't leave him, since she was 'too old and might not find anybody else on time'. Guess what? Instead, she got pregnant on purpose. He left her; he did not want babies as he had repeatedly stated for four years. Her reaction: 'If I had only known he was going to leave me.'

I should not talk about other women's stories without mentioning my own. After my daughter was born, I tried to stage a reconciliation with my father and play happy families. He flew over a couple of times with my mother, and they argued at the first opportunity. Later, he came a few times by himself. I have to admit, he tried to be nice, but it was never going to work. Abusers do not change.

One morning, when Michael was at work, my father had one of his temper fits. My daughter and I had to leave our own house. I was petrified, and Victoria told me she was very scared of the 'loud man'. We have not seen him since. I have cut all contact with him and blocked him on all my devices. Best thing I have ever done.

Charity donation

Over the years, charities that dealt with problems related to elderly people attracted my attention consistently. I was inclined to contribute more to them than to others dealing with the younger generation. I saw the golden generation as being more vulnerable than children. I perceived their age as an impediment to achieving a better quality of life; a young person still has plenty of time and energy to improve his or her life.

However, I started donating money to the NSPCC when I had my daughter because the idea that a child has their whole life in front of them to improve their chances is not necessarily true. I realised how vulnerable a child is. They are entirely in our hands. If somebody abuses a child, that child often does not have the capacity to ask for help. If they grow up in a nasty environment, some of them will be so damaged by the time they are adults that they may never find happiness.

Do you play or do you work first?

An old incident at work that had been spinning around my head for a few years finally made sense. We had one of those annoying get-together company events that I usually managed to avoid. Disappointedly, there was a catch-up day for all those other astute workers like me. When I found out who else would be attending, my heart sank. One of the women was a total disaster, a walking synonym of missing deadlines and misunderstandings. My boss was outraged at my comments regarding the quality of her work. He used to tell me off for being harsh on her.

We were all asked at this team-building exercise, 'Do you play or do you work first?'

I replied, 'I work first because I cannot enjoy playing if I have work at the back of my mind.'

The aforementioned colleague answered, 'I play first because if I had to finish work before I could play, I would never play'.

She had two small children, was working four days a week as part of her work experience while finishing her university degree, and was attending lectures on her day off. At the time, I did not understand or agree with her answer. I do now.

I wish I had not wasted so much time when I was single

When I had Victoria, I would not have changed my life

for anything – but if I could have magically gone back in time, I would have done so many things differently.

I spent fifteen years agonising because I had always wanted to study for a PhD, but I believed I was too old; it was far too late to get on with it. Was it?

I also spent ages considering whether to buy a tiny property with the help of my now deceased great aunt, who offered me a free loan. I never accepted because I was waiting to buy a bigger property with the man of my dreams. But when I met my husband, he already had his home. Later, when I had no job, no great aunt, and no properties were for sale at their former rates, one of my biggest dreams in life fell away because I did not jump for it when I had the opportunity.

When I met my husband, I was seriously considering further study. Every time I got fed up with him spending more time on Facebook than with me, I would fume upstairs and tell myself I could be studying for my MBA during the time he spent on Facebook – so why on earth did I not do it?

Do not listen to anybody – not even to this book – but make your own rules

Vulnerability was written all over me when I was pregnant and in the early stages of motherhood. Easy prey. A pregnant woman is the perfect candidate for unrequested instruction. For example, in hospital, we were forbidden to use duvets for babies. They get too hot, we were told, and there is danger of asphyxiation. On the other hand, I had my mother-in-law getting angry at me over the phone because she wanted to buy a German duvet for Victoria.

She had put her children under German duvets to sleep when they were babies; in their first house they did not have the heating on at night and using the thickest possible duvet was certainly the best thing to do in her case. She called Michael at work to complain when I told her that she was welcome to buy a German duvet for Victoria, however, in view of hospital advice, she would not be using it until she was over one year old.

I usually avoid confrontation if I can help it. When the nice post-pregnancy hormones were up, I had even less desire to have an argument and was usually too busy with the baby or too tired to bother. Instead, I was just absurdly nice to everyone. It becomes irritating and confusing when everybody has strong opinions and you are expected to do what you are told.

But no! In the end, it was my life, my body, my child. It was fine to seek advice but ultimately, I had the right to make my own decisions. If nobody criticises my choice of job, haircut, or holiday destination, why did they have to tell me about which milk to give Victoria? Or when to put her to bed or which cream to put on her bum? At least 90 per cent of my agonies of self-doubt were produced by the constant criticism and unsolicited advice of others and reading too many parenting books with too many strong opinions.

I was sure, when I had a second child, I was going to enjoy it more because I had gone through the motherhood learning-curve experience. As my neighbour – a mother of three children and grandmother of five grandchildren – said to me, it is not until you realise that your child is fine, and she is going to be fine, that you start enjoying it. It just takes *a little while* to get there.

On average, you lose five friends when you have a baby

When I was told this, I did not want to believe it. It didn't sound right. I would never abandon a friend who became a mother. Sadly, it has turned out to be true for me. On the one hand, I no longer have the time to travel to see my friends abroad. However, there is no nastiness on either side: the situation simply cannot be helped. On the other hand, some of my single friends, haunted by the desire of getting a baby of their own, stopped being around.

Once you have a baby, you may find that many of your old friends assume that mums are obsessed with talking about their baby, which is 100 per cent true from their point of view and in a way tragically true from your own view, because, as a friend of mine with a little baby once told me, 'I don't do anything else with my life – it is all about the baby. There is no physical time for anything else.' Therefore, a conversation with a single woman with a fast and loud biological ticking clock can become difficult.

I used to know somebody who I considered a good friend. She was a high-flier and one of those types who'd go gleefully to work almost every Sunday to show off her dedication to the firm. She was always bitter about maternity rights, altogether angry that she had to pay taxes for 'lazy mothers to stay at home with their babies'. Well, she refused to talk to me once I got pregnant.

No need to despair, though: true friends will stay with you, even if for a while you will not see much of them. In due course, you will make new friends at the school gates.

Your professional life will change 100 per cent, but your husband's will remain the same, sorry about the unfair generalisation on some husbands

Having a baby has been the biggest change in my life. Nothing compared to when I moved countries by myself, at the time not even owning a mobile phone or having an email address. I changed careers several times, from humble beginnings as a sale assistant in a chocolate shop, sharing a room with two American girls, where a leak from the bathroom upstairs dripped directly onto my pillow, to becoming a web manager. A few years before that, I had stopped working for a while to become a full-time masters student in Edinburgh and then moved in with my boyfriend and finally got married. None of those events compared to having a child.

I used to urge couples to have children before having my own. Afterwards, I changed my message: 'Think about it! It has to be done at the right time for you; more importantly, are you ready to sacrifice virtually everything else?' I have always thought Victoria was the best thing in my life. However, I should have been better prepared.

I find it easier to tell the truth to anybody who wonders why we have only one child, rather than keep it to myself. I'd rather talk about my lost babies than keep quiet as if they were a shameful secret. I wonder sometimes what they would be like and what they would like to eat or play with.

When reading articles about women who have had multiple miscarriages, I understand now why they kept on trying, when before I would have asked, 'Was not once enough pain? Isn't it time to move on?' There is only one way to overcome a miscarriage, and it is with a successful pregnancy. Anything else is hard to accept.

I do not think about them every day, or at least I try not to – but it is difficult when writing a book about it. It has taken me years to go to bed and not dedicate my last dream of the day to having a second baby; of being in the operating theatre again and hearing the doctor saying, 'Put the curtain down', and seeing the baby for the first time. One day it will get easier. I will never forget them, though, because I do not want to.

In the end, were my struggles to have another child worth the pain and suffering, emotionally and physically?

Would my husband and I have gone ahead if we had known then what we know now? It's impossible to say. However hard it has been, ours has been a journey lit by hope – and while it has undoubtedly been challenging in every respect, I am glad that we gave it our all.

I look forward in my life. We cannot change our past, only our future.

ABOUT THE AUTHOR

Ellie Roberts was born in Spain. She has spent half of her life living in England. She has had a colourful career that includes being an aerobics instructor, chocolate shop manager, web developer, and web manager. This is her first book. She currently lives in Guildford with her family and dogs.

www.ingramcontent.com/pod-product-compliance
Lightning Source LLC
Chambersburg PA
CBHW070546050426
42450CB00027B/2748